DISCOVERING
BURIED WORLDS

DISCOVERING
BURIED WORLDS

ANDRÉ PARROT

Curator-in-Chief of the French National Museums,
Professor at the Ecole du Louvre, Paris,
Director of the Mari Archaeological Expedition

PHILOSOPHICAL LIBRARY

NEW YORK

Translated by Edwin Hudson

from the French

DÉCOUVERTE DES MONDES ENSEVELIS

(Delachaux and Niestlé, Neuchâtel 1954)

First English language edition July 1955

Published 1955, by the Philosophical Library, Inc.,
15 East 40th Street, New York, 16, N.Y.

Printed in Great Britain for Philosophical Library, Inc., by
The Northumberland Press Limited, Gateshead on Tyne

CONTENTS

LIST OF ILLUSTRATIONS

(placed between pp. 64-65)

MAPS

PREFACE TO THE
SECOND EDITION

RETURNING to France from my ninth campaign of
excavations at Mari (October-December 1953), I learn
that the first edition of *Découverte des mondes ensevelis*
is exhausted, and I am asked to allow a second impression to be made without alteration to the text.

The reception given to the book prompts me to change
nothing of what I have written. To those who have at
times expressed regret at the very minor place given to
Egypt, my answer is two-fold. Firstly, I wished to con-
fine myself in this book to what I knew at first hand. I
believe that actual personal experiences are infinitely
more interesting to the reader than excursions into fields
where the author must necessarily be dependent on the
work of others. Secondly, Egypt will certainly not be
absent from the *Studies*, where it will be given the
important place which is its due. But we must not rush
ahead too fast, and I prefer to begin where my ignorance
is least.

The criticisms I have read have likewise encouraged
me to remain faithful to the spirit in which I
endeavoured, as an introduction to the *Studies in Biblical
Archaeology*, to define the problem and sketch its outlines. I have tried to do so frankly and sincerely. It is
exactly twenty-seven years since I started my first
excavation in the Middle East. By now I might be either

blasé or bored. But I find archaeological excavation more fascinating than ever.

Three weeks ago my workmen's picks were beginning to reveal fresh 'buried' treasures, which lack of time forced us to cover up again after only a glimpse : fresh monuments, a considerable architecture, hidden beneath tons of rubbish. I shall, God willing, exhume them just as all the others have been cleared.

It is fascinating, exciting work—tiring, too, for the task becomes increasingly complex as one becomes aware of the incalculable importance of these records which are re-emerging into the light of day. They are important not only for a better understanding of the history and culture of near-eastern civilization, but because of the powerful light which they throw upon the religion and beliefs of a people in search of the supernatural forces which dominate them and on which they depend.

During this last compaign at Mari we have found more figures with hands joined in an attitude of worship. Since there have been men, men who pray, this has been for them the only possible attitude. This new and moving lesson comes to us once more across the ages, and it is a lesson which we must share with others. I hope that this book will in some small way contribute to that sharing. That was my object in writing it, and to that end I leave it in the hands of fresh readers, among whom I am confident, the past being the pledge of the future, that I shall find new and trusted friends.

Paris
  1st January 1954

INTRODUCTION

BURIED WORLDS, that is literally what the explorers of to-day are reconquering. Most of these ancient towns, destroyed by wars and eroded by time, had disappeared. Their ruins had little by little been covered up by the sand of the desert and the grass and scrub of the wilderness. Thus renowned cities had vanished, their very names often forgotten.

There came a day when men determined to find them again. In the forefront of this enterprise, France, with her diplomats, her travellers and pioneers, boldly pointed the way. Soon other countries followed, joining the French in this work, but never surpassing them. After a century of effort the balance-sheet is an impressive one.

The museums of Europe, the Near East and the New World have become the guardians of these precious relics. But do those who contemplate them in ever-increasing numbers hear the authentic echo of those voices from the past? How many there are who pass them by with but the most cursory of glances! If they do not feel, perhaps it is because they do not know, lacking the indispensable initiation. It is true that these worlds which the archaeologist and the historian have brought back from oblivion seem remote and very different from our own. Yet who would dare to claim that western civilization is not the heir of the civilizations of the Near East, succeeding to their heritage of art and

[11]

culture, the inventory of which is now being made?
Who would deny our debt to the peoples of the Nile
valley or the banks of the Euphrates? Are there not in
the East inexhaustible treasures waiting to be revealed
to the scholar, the artist and the believer? How can
we forget that it is to the Sumerians that we owe, among
other things, the sexagesimal system, and to the
Phoenicians our alphabet? Can we stand unmoved
beneath the six columns of Baalbek or at the door of
the tombs at Petra? What shall we say if it is granted
us to penetrate the thoughts of the ancients, and to turn
over the leaves of their antique archives? If, in short,
we come to sit and warm ourselves by that fire which,
never quite dead under its ashes, is being fanned anew
by attentive hands?

In these desert lands the explorers have advanced.
Under the excavator's pick age-old civilizations have
reappeared. They were thought to be dead. They were
only sleeping.

Paris
   15th September 1952

I

THE BURIED CITY
RE-EMERGES

THE TRAVELLER who disembarks in the Near East
finds that the past asserts itself at once, but not everywhere with the same intensity, nor, above all, with equal
vividness. This need not surprise us : there are degrees
in the impressions we experience. Karnak by moon-
light or the Ramesseum amid the long shadows of a
January afternoon arouse an emotion quite different
from that which one feels before the six columns
of Baalbek or the door of 'Belshazzar's palace' at
Babylon.

Undoubtedly the architectural style differs, even
though the monuments are all on a colossal scale, but
that does not altogether explain these varying and sometimes opposite reactions. The setting comes into play
and gives the tone. One cannot forget the tawny screen
of the desert cliff which follows the Nile, or the lofty
yellow-brown line of Mount Lebanon, where, under the
violent blue of the sky, white trails of snow linger
tenaciously on late into the year. It is against this
cliff that the Ramesseum raises its harmonious columns,
and at the foot of Mount Lebanon that Baalbek spreads
the proud glory of its gigantic ruins. At Babylon, the
contrast is complete. Not far from the line of palms
along the ribbon of the Euphrates, the great dilapidated

heaps of disembowelled palaces lie under the blazing sun, which for nine months out of the twelve annuls every architectural detail. These grey bricks are cheerless compared with the golden limestone of Phoenicia or the rose-coloured granite of Aswan. Nevertheless the visitor is aware of overtones of great memories, and an accompaniment—one might say an orchestration—of mighty names: Hammurabi, Nebuchadnezzar; without them this desolate place might seem bleak and disenchanted. But we may as well admit that it is disappointing to find that very little is left at Babylon of the 'hanging gardens', and practically nothing of the 'Tower of Babel'.

However, the ruins of Thebes, Baalbek and Babylon are accessible enough to figure on the tourist itineraries. Here, where the architecture is on the surface, even the uninitiated can enter into contact with the visible past. But how many there are who pass unsuspectingly by a world still buried! In Mesopotamia the monotony of desert or plain is broken here and there by folds in the ground dominated by a few low hills. The inexperienced traveller, hurrying along the track, would be most surprised to learn that he had passed within a few yards of a dead city. In Upper Syria, or in that astonishingly fertile plain called Al Jazira, on the left bank of the Euphrates, we no longer find these long folds, but instead a single enormous mass of earth, called a *tell*, rising from the surrounding plain like a huge blister. Here too a town is hidden, more compact than the other. At its foot modern houses, looking like beehives with their conical roofs, are constructed from the rubble of buildings several thousand years old (Plate 1).

In this country nature is often harsh. She takes vengeance from time to time on our civilization which has brought its machines and its technology to a soil which for long ages tolerated only the feet of camels or at most the solid wheels of chariots. There are sandstorms, and quicksands in the moving dunes, ordeals seldom avoided by travellers crossing certain parts of southern Iraq. In complete contrast, there is the vengeance of the mud, when, after the heavy winter rains, the desert is turned for several days into an impassable swamp, in which motor-cars, caught by the bad weather, sink to the axles. There they must remain, if help is not at hand, until the ground has dried out sufficiently for them to be extricated.

But the severe climate has never discouraged anyone: rather the contrary. We really appreciate only the things we have striven for, and the crossing of the desert has ceased to be a difficulty, now that motor-buses ply over its well-marked tracks, and the pipelines pierce its heart. There is, however, a great contrast between the stony plain and the charm of the river banks. The vast and desolate solitudes give way to vegetation, trees and fields. Coming from Syria into Iraq, one sees at first only sparsely scattered palm-trees. Gradually they become more numerous, and soon the traveller is passing through immense gardens, cool and shady oases, where amid the splashing of the norias he may rest from sun and dust, and taste to the full the delights of an earthly paradise. Out there in the desert he felt discouraged and weary, but now his trials are all forgotten and life smiles upon him once more. As one wanders among the palm-groves of Anah, Hilla or Basra it is easy to imagine that one is in that 'garden planted eastward in Eden' of the Book of Genesis.

It is not surprising that tradition placed Paradise there, nor that great empires were able to flourish there. On the main traffic-route of the ancient world, between the Persian Gulf and the Mediterranean, looking at once towards India and towards the West, Mesopotamia lay at the heart of civilization. That civilization, after shining with incomparable lustre, faded, and then was extinguished. It lies there, beneath those mounds of debris which the picks of the archaeologists have begun to clear away.

*   *   *

An archaeological exploration, however small, must be planned down to the last detail. When one is to live for several months in the open desert, it is advisable to draw up a list of everything necessary for the life and work of an expedition which will find nothing or next to nothing in the sector where its camp is to be established. But isolation is not always complete. The following examples are drawn from my own experience:

At Byblos, where I assisted M. Dunand in 1928, the bazaars were within a stone's throw of the excavations, supplying all the provisions we wanted. At Baalbek in 1927 our comfort was even greater: we ate and slept at the hotel. At Nerab, my first excavation (1926), we were indeed in tents, but from the *tell* we could see the citadel of Aleppo, a bare five miles away. Every Sunday I had 'twenty-four hours' leave' to go into the town and enjoy the pleasures of civilization.

[16]

Fortunately, not all the sites are so easily accessible, and it is here, in an isolation which may be complete, that our most vivid memories are formed. At Tello, whose approaches have become impracticable for cars, we were nevertheless not really alone, for around the ruins was a ring of encampments, at a distance of from three to six miles from our own camp. At Mari, Abu Kemal is only seven miles away, but there are villages even nearer, and with the development of irrigation there are fields right up to the foot of the *tells*. Larsa (Plate 2), is the ideal place for a cure of silence and meditation. Here is the true desert, with not a single encampment in sight. All around, sand-dunes encircle the plain, blackened here and there with stunted clumps of tamarisk. There is a pool of unpleasant brackish water at the bottom of a hole dug by passing Bedouins on the move with their flocks. The nearest revictualling and postal facilities are thirty miles away, and when I was there (in 1933), available only once a week.

Such experiences leave an indelible impression on one who has heard the call of the desert. Living in that austere setting, linked with civilization and with home by the weekly arrival of a bundle of mail—from which the letter one particularly wants is sometimes missing— and a few newspapers, usually a fortnight old, one feels called to live life as it should be lived, honestly, without conventions and prejudices. One engages in an unremitting struggle against the elements and against fauna of many different kinds : the sun, for it is merciless in this shadeless land; the rain, fortunately infrequent, which turns the camp into a prison, for the mud is a more effective barrier than the thickest barbed-wire entangle-

[17]

ment; the heat of the early afternoon, when it would often be so much pleasanter to enjoy a siesta than to go up to the excavations; at night the cold invades the *zarifas*, our huts made of reeds which are like ovens at midday and ice-houses at midnight; the vicious and offensive flies; the scorpions which crawl at the foot of the walls and sometimes conceal themselves in one's bed-clothes; the horned vipers (Plate 3) lurking in the rubble of the ruins, whose bite would be fatal in a matter of minutes even to the most robust victim.

It is a struggle without quarter, which shows up man as he really is, his failings accentuated as his nerves are stretched, but also revealing possibilities and resources which increase in proportion to the efforts he is called upon to make in order to fulfil his mission. Such a life not only strengthens a man physically and morally, but also brings spiritual enrichment. In the silence of the desert, broken only by the wailing of jackals and the howling of hyenas, when the camp lies hushed beneath the nightly splendour of the starry vault of the heavens, a man's soul opens wide to the breath of the infinite, and learns the lesson of eternity. It is in the desert at night that one should re-read Psalm 19:

The heavens declare the glory of God;
And the firmament sheweth his handywork.
Day unto day uttereth speech,
And night unto night sheweth knowledge.[1]

In the silence of the night also, the past seems to come nearer. Among the ruins, where walls and angles show

[1] vv. 1-2.

faintly against the darker shadows, one expects at any moment to see reappearing those who, four or five thousand years ago, trod the same soil, opened their breasts to the same cool breeze, and counted the same stars. But in the morning the mirage has vanished. The labourers come in from all directions to re-form their teams and set to work. Picks begin once more to bite into the soil.

* * *

From sunrise to sunset, with a long break at midday and shorter pauses in the middle of the morning and afternoon, two hundred, sometimes three hundred when work is in full swing, are employed. Our tools are heavy picks and shovels, and small tip-wagons. Porters carry the freshly dug soil in baskets from the excavation to the wagon. At the beginning of each campaign, when everyone is still untrained, a period of ' running-in ' is necessary. But the strong-armed Bedouin soon learns to handle a pick, and the unsteady legs of the boys quickly adapt themselves to the endless shuttling back and forth between the pick and the wagon. At the end of each day an impressive volume of earth has been dug out and transported, basketful by basketful, to be heaped in giant cones as far away as possible, preferably right outside the *tells*, so as not to cover up areas of archaeological interest that may be excavated in their own turn at some future date.

Once the surface layer has been removed, walls appear. They are easy to follow if built of stone or baked brick, but difficult to distinguish when the building material—the more perishable sun-dried brick or puddled clay—blends with the surrounding earth. More often than not the ancient constructions have crumbled, worn by the elements and shattered by war and pillage. Then progress is slow, and sometimes smaller tools must be used. Frequent pauses are necessary, to allow the earth to dry, so that by its different colouring what is artificial may be distinguished from what is not. The reader will see that excavation has a technique all its own, which may not be learnt from books, but only from actual experience on the archaeological site. The technique has been greatly improved over the last twenty years. Its aim is to reduce to a minimum the damage done, so that the excavator will not be destroying for ever the very thing he is seeking.

* * *

This task, which becomes increasingly complicated as one approaches the totally unknown, needs a whole team of experts, who form the ' staff ' of the expedition, under a director who is the brains and the driving force. The size of the team depends on the financial resources available. Each member has his clearly defined function.

The surveyor plots all the structures as they appear. The draughtsman keeps a marked plan showing every object of note (statuettes, pottery, tools, baked clay objects, jewels, amulets and so on). The photographer, as the campaign advances, must compile an ever-increasing and permanent record on plate and reel of everything already noted by the surveyor and the draughtsman, and in addition many things outside their province, such as the progress of the work and the actual uncovering of objects. The epigraphist deciphers as rapidly as possible every written document that comes to light, for the information thus gained may lead to a better conduct of the researches being made, and a more accurate interpretation of the results so far obtained. Attached to the expedition is an inspector representing the Department of Antiquities of the country in whose territory the excavations are taking place. Finally, the clerk of the works deals with the practical side of the excavations, the formation of gangs of labourers, the distribution and care of tools, the laying of the narrow-gauge rails for the wagons, and the dividing-up into sectors of the area under investigation.

There you have the essential framework of a typical expedition. It may, of course, be enlarged by the addition of archaeological assistants, repairers of antique objects, and technicians to help with the difficult finds necessitating special methods of extrication or consolidation. Such is the machinery whose good and harmonious functioning is one of the conditions of success, for if it is well-conducted an excavation ought always to be successful. Even on a poor site, of which there are inevitably some among the hundreds of *tells* scattered over Syria and Iraq, it is always the past that we are rediscovering, and of that past *nothing* is unimportant. Nevertheless every excavator hopes that some day fortune will smile on him, and that he too will experience the excitement of making a great discovery. Perhaps, after scraping together a few meagre vestiges of some ancient habitation, he will see the shoulder of a statue appearing, or the outlines of a palace emerging from the soil. After all, although the whole of the past is worthy of attention, some things are obviously more interesting than others.

* * *

I must admit that good fortune has attended us every year at Mari. Let me note here some of the ways in which that fortune has led us on, so as to give would-be explorers some idea of a few of our most memorable days.

Putting side by side the photograph (Plate 4) taken on our arrival, which shows exactly what the site was like before the first pick was wielded on it, and that taken after three or four campaigns (Plate 5), one can see the astonishing progress that was made. One can bring a calmer judgment to bear on those inevitable periods of disappointment and even of apprehension, when unforeseen circumstances retarded our progress, or when we drew a blank just at the point at which we had thought a discovery certain.

The fine aerial photographs taken by Aviation Française du Levant give some idea of the great size of the palace of Mari, which covers an area of more than seven acres : a veritable town within a town. Discovered in 1935, it was found to be in an astonishingly good state of preservation.

In the parts which had suffered least, the walls still rose to a height of some ten to fifteen feet. Large earthenware jars, scarcely damaged at all in spite of the weight of rubble that had covered them, stood in rows on the terracotta flagstones of vast courtyards. A stone plinth showed where a seat had stood, probably used by the steward whose duty it was to check the issue and receipt of all the assignments in kind necessary to the daily life of a large number of people. The palace must certainly have housed, as well as the royal family, the 'civil and military households', and the offices which would correspond to-day to the various ministries of State. We had no difficulty in recognizing the king's private apartments. They had been placed at one corner of the building, isolated and well protected. Thus the king and his family could live in complete privacy, away from prying eyes. Bedrooms, bathrooms with baths in place and ready for use, reception-rooms, a courtyard for relaxation and games—nothing was missing. But by the time we arrived the furniture had almost entirely disappeared, no doubt destroyed or carried off as booty by the Babylonian conquerors of the town.

Elsewhere it seemed as if life had only just stopped. One room was equipped as a kitchen. Constructed of fire-clay, with places for the cauldrons and openings for fireplaces, it could have been put into use at once. Nor would dishes be lacking, since there was a 'table-service' of almost fifty pieces, hollow vessels of varying shape and decoration, which must have been used for preparing and serving cheeses and milk products. Clearly care was taken to delight the eye at the royal table.

So we advanced through rooms, halls and courtyards. On all sides new revelations awaited us, not all equally significant, but always unpredictable. Often when we confidently anticipated a find, the search would prove fruitless, the removal of several tons of earth yielding nothing at all. Elsewhere, when we had envisaged only a sterile and tedious clearing-away of debris, *it* was there. Here, on one of the steps of a staircase, a magnificent alabaster head, its smiling profile still intact (Plate 6). There, almost on the surface, the headless statue of a governor of the town, draped in his scalloped robe, savagely mutilated on that fatal day when Hammurabi's soldiers stormed the palace and, laying about them with their maces, smashed the works of art which it housed.

Amidst what confusion must the palace have blazed as excited warriors lit a bonfire in the throne-room, heaping upon it everything they found in the adjoining rooms. Among the ashes of that fire we recognized the charred remains of huge timbers torn from the flat roofs.

In that same throne-room a majestic staircase gave access to a gallery, no doubt meant for the statue of some deity. Face upward at the foot of the stairs lay the large and almost undamaged statue of one of the local rulers (Plate 7). A brief three-line inscription carved on the shoulder gave his name and title : Ishtup-ilum, Governor of Mari. With what eager excitement did we decipher it, to learn the identity of that bearded figure with hands joined in the time-honoured attitude of the devotee before his god. Our workmen had had to lay aside their tools, and they watched my late beloved colleague André Bianquis (d. 3rd April 1936) as he took a pick and set to work to disengage the heavy sculpture from its sheath of earth, which was left marked with the massive imprint. The task took several hours, but his efforts were finally crowned with complete success.

André Bianquis also had the honour of unearthing at Mari the first cuneiform tablets. Heaped together was an impressive accumulation of archives: contracts, inventories of merchandise, lists of men and women workers, accounts, but especially the diplomatic correspondence of a court and State of the beginning of the second millennium B.C. These thousands of texts have been entrusted to a team of French and Belgian Assyriologists (among whom I am pleased to be able to quote the names of Messrs. Jean, Kupper, Bottéro, Finet, Boyer, Jestin and Birot) under the direction of Professor G. Dossin. They are being published by the French State Press under the title *Archives royales de Mari*. Up to the present five volumes of the long series have been published, and it is hoped to produce two further collections each year. Thus in the shortest possible time we shall have made known this new world, so suddenly rediscovered in all its aspects—political, geographical, economic and juridical.

But it is not only history in this broad sense that comes to life again as we read those little clay tablets, engraved on both sides with a stiletto in close unbroken lines. We can read there also the lesser history of daily life, with its everyday happenings and its interesting titbits of information, for alongside the graven reports of envoys, ambassadors, governors and military leaders, there are the private letters, notes from a wife to her husband, letters from a sister to her brother, and epistles from father to son or son to father. Thus, Shiptu, wife of King Zimrilim and hence Queen of Mari, with tender solicitude urges her lord and master to keep himself well covered up during the journey he is undertaking, so as not to catch cold. Moreover, like any other dutiful and loving wife, she sends him some warm clothing.

Such are the men and women who move across the stage of that ancient world. Reading the tablets we seem sometimes to hear their voices, and we long to be able to see them, to fit faces to all the personalities, the details of whose lives we are gradually piecing together.

If certain of the ancient statues are portraits, we can indeed contemplate the actual features of a few of the important dignitaries of the city, since some of the sculptures bear illustrious names: Lamgi-Mari, King of Mari, Ebih-il the steward, Idi-narum the miller, Ishtup-ilum, Governor of Mari (Plate 8).

But a portrait, however faithful, is not the same thing as the original, and that the excavator will find only in an untouched tomb. However, there are no mummies in Mesopotamia, as there are in Egypt, where the death-mask—like that, for instance, of Seti I—is so impressive when the technique of embalming has preserved it from corruption.

In the graves which we have discovered, the skeletons are sometimes shrouded in what was once the skin of an animal or a cloth. Often, when the coffin has not been completely sealed, they are embedded in earth which has filtered through. There follows the delicate task of clearing this soil away from the body without disturbing its arrangement, firstly in order to note its exact position, and secondly to make a detailed record of the articles which were usually buried with the dead person.

Burials are of various types according to the period and, of course, the social position of the individual. An important necropolis of the Seleucid period (fourth-first centuries B.C.) was discovered intact at Mari in 1951.

Some of the bodies were enclosed in coffins of baked clay shaped like walnut-shells, others in huge jars cut away at the side to facilitate the introduction of the corpse.

At the beginning of the first millennium B.C. the Assyrians had a military colony at Mari, acting as an occupation force to hold a bridgehead on the right bank of the Euphrates, and at the same time to control the great caravan route between the Persian Gulf and the Mediterranean. Their burial-grounds, discovered in 1936 and 1951, had been placed among the ruins of buildings over a thousand years old. The tombs were immediately recognizable from the characteristic practice of placing two large jars together mouth to mouth. A space of just over five feet was thus enclosed, and in this the body was placed on its side with knees bent.

In order to open the grave without damage, the soil must first be cleared from around the jars, which are then cut open lengthwise. The pieces thus detached are removed, and then the excavator must work patiently with small tools—a trowel, a moulder's spoon, and frequently an artist's brush—clearing away the earth which has filtered through. Little by little the body reappears as it was left some three thousand years ago, surrounded by its treasures (Plate 9). Here lies a great lady, her forehead adorned with a diadem of precious stones set in gold, a gold ring in her nose, wearing earrings with milled edges, and rings and bracelets on her hands and arms. On her breast lies a curious mask of glazed frit representing the face of a youth. Disposed about her are containers for sweetmeats, pitchers, flagons, and a bronze mirror. In accordance with some mysterious rite, on each knee rests an ostrich egg. Not far away is another grave, evidently that of a soldier, for as well as the vessels and trinkets there lies beside the skeleton a bronze quiver containing iron darts.

Some thousand years earlier the procedure of burial is the same, the only difference being in the coffin. Again one finds two receptacles mouth to mouth, but instead of being laid flat they have been placed almost vertical. The funeral furniture is frequently composed of pottery disposed around the outside. But a kind of vat-sarcophagus of the same period has also been found. In this the body is laid horizontally, though still curled up.

Several centuries before this the coffins are still of baked clay (Plate 10). The corpse lies either under a sort of lid, or else in two receptacles ornamented with thick ribs and placed mouth to mouth, the joint being reinforced with flat bricks. It seems to have been the custom to bury the bodies of children all together in one spot, under the flooring at the foot of one of the walls of the house. As with the adults, their coffins were of baked clay. In place of the usual jar a sort of vase was used, covered with a bowl or a large plate. The little body, disjointed though it was, had nevertheless with it a modest funeral equipment: one or two goblets and a few animal bones for nourishment in the beyond. Thus did the Mesopotamians lay to rest those who had entered 'the house of no return'.

* * *

This existence after death, though it inspired apprehension and even dread, was not considered as an automatic reward for good and evil done on earth. Nor does the after-life appear to have been thought of as in any way dependent on personal beliefs or faith. And yet men lived from the cradle to the grave under the protection of a powerful pantheon, in which they believed and to whom they offered regular sacrifices. Their whole life was lived in the presence of these beneficent beings. Ample testimony of all this is furnished by the numerous temples discovered and by the valuable documentary evidence generally found in them. Only the officiating priests and the faithful worshippers are missing, but it is not hard to imagine them.

The existence in some of these religious cults of mysterious ceremonies, in which only the initiated (priests and rulers) might take part, is implied by certain architectural and decorative features. Entry to the sanctuary was restricted by zig-zag doorways and narrow passages, while outside bronze lions, jaws menacingly open and bodies crouched ready to spring, stood guard over who knows what awful rites within. The temple of Dagon at Mari was protected by rows of such beasts outside on the parade and again inside the building. We may be sure that the guard they mounted was not considered as merely symbolic, but as real and active.

We know that the setting-up of the lions was regarded as a memorable event, since one year of King Zimrilim's reign is dated from the installation of the lions at the door of the temple of Dagon. It was also the final act in the construction and consecration of the sanctuary. Every phase of the work had been accompanied by the meticulous performance of rites whose object was to ensure that the deity would accept the house without reserve when finally men solemnly offered it to him. For if men have their houses, ought not the god to have his? In one of these ceremonies a foundation-deposit was buried at a corner of the building, a rite comparable in all respects with that of the 'foundation-stone' of our own day.

We have already found many of these deposits at Mari. Several have been discovered at the corners of the temples of Ishtar and Ninharsag, three at three of the corners of the temple of Dagon (the fourth, which we were confident of finding, has so far eluded all our researches); two others, on either side of the door-sill of a building called a *sahuru*; and one more at the heart of the solid mass of the archaic *ziggurat* located in 1952. This last was identical with those of the temple of Ishtar: a copper nail driven vertically through a flat-collared peg and surrounded by uninscribed tablets of stone and silver. This reticence is difficult to understand, since the Mesopotamian builders generally vied with each other in repeating their own names and that of the deity they wished to honour. Fortunately, at the beginning of the second millennium this reserve gave way to greater candour. In the deposits of the temples of Dagon and Ninharsag we found names of governors or princes who had erected them: Niwar-Mer, Apil-kin, Ishme-Dagon, Ishtup-ilum. The last named was none other than the prince whose statue we had found in 1935 lying in the throne-room.

In these once well-guarded sanctuaries a rich hoard often awaits the archaeologist, at least when it has not been located by conquerors or robbers in ancient times. Nor must I omit to mention the illicit diggers who, in modern times, have, as at Khafajah, frequently preceded the official excavators and cheated them of valuable finds and archaeological information. When, however, one is fortunate enough to be the first on the scene, one often reaps a harvest rich indeed. Such was our good fortune at Mari in 1939 in the temple of Ishtar, while in the previous year we found a smaller and considerably less valuable store in the temple of Ninharsag. I cannot say the same for the few scattered relics we picked up in 1952, in the temples that back on to the ancient *ziggurat*, for in the past they had been almost completely devastated.

Now and again votive offerings are included, statuettes of male and female worshippers (Plate 12), left more than four thousand five hundred years ago on the sanctuary ledges. In the mind of the donors they were to prolong prayer and adoration in the same way as candles while they burn represent the presence of the faithful.

In January 1934 we picked them up by the dozen in the ruins of a building we were unable at first to identify. For several days we came upon them one after another. One of them was of capital importance, for it was to furnish us with the name of the town on which we had been working for six weeks. It was when we picked up the little white statue inscribed with the name of a king of Mari (Plate 11, left) that all at once we realized that Tell Hariri was in reality the dynastic city of Mari, and that the structure we were uncovering was the temple of the goddess Ishtar, in whose honour the faithful had

[31]

brought their statuettes, jewels, weapons and precious vases. Gifts had been left there not only by the inhabitants of the city, but also by pilgrims who had perhaps crossed the desert in order to prostrate themselves at the feet of the deity, who, among other attributes, was the goddess of fertility, of love and of war. Her star was the Evening and the Morning Star, and thus she was considered both as a morning goddess, in which rôle she marked the hour of battle, and a goddess of the evening, the time when fighting ceases and men seek in sweeter encounters to forget the din of the battlefield. The Ishtar of Mari had two aspects, but nevertheless it seems that with her, warlike exploits took precedence over the pleasures of the senses, for in texts which refer to her she receives the curious epithet ' virile '.

To ' virile Ishtar ' of Mari, men and women of every degree had dedicated statuettes of gypsum or alabaster. When, after the season's work, they were gathered together and classified, they constituted an oddly impressive assembly, some without bodies, others without heads (Plate 12). Those few figures that had remained whole seemed to be calling on some invisible jury to witness their surprise at having come unscathed through such a massacre!

*　　　*　　　*

The palace at Mari, the temples of Ishtar, Dagon and Ninharsag, and the *ziggurat*, are the richest structures that I have excavated, both in the quality of their architecture and in the number and beauty of the sculptures found there. Mesopotamian art, generally believed to be

[32]

rigid and even brutal, here presents a more genial countenance. Yet another revelation was in store for us in the form of mural paintings dating from the beginning of the second millennium. Until the discovery of Mari the only pictorial documentation we possessed (as far as ancient western Asia was concerned) was of much later date, having been found in Assyrian palaces (eighth century B.C.), in the temples of Greek and Oriental gods and in the Christian Church at Dura-Europus (third century A.D.), and in Phoenician and Palmyrene tombs (first-third centuries A.D.). With the Mari paintings we step back in time at least a thousand years.

The unearthing of these compositions was no easy task. Frequently we found them smashed into thousands of tiny fragments and scattered about in the debris. Nothing of them could have been saved had it not been for the genius and patience of my surveyor-draughtsman Paul François, who died on 3rd April 1936, in the same tragic accident that carried off his comrade André Bianquis. It was he who collected them, fragment by fragment, and fitted them together like a jigsaw puzzle. A careful study of the result afforded a fairly clear impression of the general composition.

Another fine painting was by good fortune discovered *in situ*, near a doorway, where it decorated the façade of a courtyard. Unhappily the conflagration which devastated the palace had noticeably darkened the colouring. We were nevertheless able to reclaim it. Mr. H. Pearson, a first-rate specialist in the removal of ancient frescoes, with the assistance of our clerk of the works, M. G. Tellier, carried out the operation, which consisted of removing a thin painted film from the mud wall. Some years later the salts used in the ancient pigment were found to be so unstable that it was only with difficulty that modern chemists found a means of preserving them.

Clearly, archaeologists must exercise the greatest care in saving from destruction what their picks have disinterred, for it is then that the danger is often greatest. The protective covering of earth or sand once removed, light and air return immediately to the attack. The least one can do is to compile a detailed report, with line-drawings and sketches in colour checked by photographs. When the work of the archaeologist has finished, that of the museum curator begins.

*   *   *

I have attempted so far to give some idea of the work of a big horizontal excavation, the object of which is to uncover a whole complex of ruined buildings over a wide area. Examples of this type of work can be seen on most excavation sites, revealing habitations grouped, much as in our own day, in streets and districts.

It is obvious that the archaeologist cannot restrict himself to area-excavation, since he would be confined to only one period of history. It is known that ancient towns are often superimposed one upon another. It frequently happened that a town was destroyed; but then life began again : the site would be summarily levelled, and reconstruction would begin above the previous dwellings. Thus, as the archaeologist digs below the surface levels into the depths of the *tell*, he reaches further and further back into time. The ideal would be to clear and remove the whole town, stratum by stratum. In the case of these Mesopotamian capitals the task would be impossibly expensive, and would occupy several lifetimes. Besides, the results would not justify the effort expended.

Nevertheless, no modern excavator can neglect this journey back into time. He chooses therefore a restricted sector where he will be able to dig down to ' natural soil '—soil, that is, which bears no further trace of human occupation—or at least to the water table, at which investigation must cease even though the level of natural soil has not been reached.

This is always fascinating work. One has the feeling of slowly pushing back the gates of the unknown. History ceases at the point where there are no more written documents, and we pass into proto-history, in which the phases of man's existence and of civilization are to be reckoned in long periods which are difficult to date, although we do at least know the order in which they succeeded one another. At these levels the excavator can expect little in the way of works of art. Yet every detail is of value and must be carefully recorded.

Each day the great trench with its massed teams of workmen grows a little deeper, and the stairways lengthen. These have at first been planned to be fairly wide (Plate 13) in order to speed up the evacuation of earth and give free passage to the lines of porters. Afterwards they have to be made narrower, and the labourers set to work to halve them (Plate 14). The file of porters moves more slowly, but still the earth is removed, basket by basket. The moment comes when the water table is reached, and the trench is turned into a quagmire. There one must stop, unless pumps are available to draw the water out. At Tello we were compelled to stop at fifty-five feet, although we had not reached the limit of human occupation. Having started from the surface 'in about the year 3000', we had gone back in this way over at least a thousand years.

We endeavoured to learn what we could from the scattered objects we dug up. Billhooks of hard-baked clay spoke of cultivation and crops; small weights suggested fishing-nets, while bent earthenware nails had no doubt been used to fix the reed matting on the walls and roofs of primitive dwellings; axes might be the weapons of the hunter, and at the same time the tools of the cultivator or the equipment of the fighter. Spindles indicated spinning and weaving. Rings made of shell or earthenware had long since fallen from the fingers they must once have adorned, while the grinder for making cosmetics tells of how humanity has from the beginning affected to improve on Nature. The earliest pottery bore a decoration in bold brush-strokes which consisted of varied animal and geometrical shapes, often ingeniously executed. Are these the beginnings of art, a conventional language, marks to indicate ownership, or magical signs? It is impossible to say with any certainty.

These relics have little intrinsic value, yet with them we have come to the very earliest stages of 'civilization'. Has that civilization a message for us? It is hard to believe that those who lit the flame did not sometimes think of those who were to pick it up and pass it on in the future. It is a far cry from the clay sickle to the atomic pile. One wonders if men were happier!

II

THE SAGA OF THE
ARCHAEOLOGISTS

(1842-1952)

I SHALL say nothing here of the travellers and traders who, from the time of Herodotus onwards, journeyed in the Orient, although their accounts of their travels are often of more than passing interest. There can be no doubt that Napoleon's Egyptian Expedition of 1798 marks a turning point in the resurrection of the past. To the expeditionary force, which was commanded by thirty-one of Bonaparte's ablest generals, was attached a whole galaxy of scholars—one hundred and sixty-five members of the Commission of Sciences and Arts, according to figures recently quoted by Pierre Vendryès in his *De la probabilité en Histoire*.

While the troops of the Directory were driving back the Mamelukes, the civilians set to work on a documentation of the visible monuments which was to serve as a basis for a magnificent *Description de l'Egypte*. Published in 1809, this great work was the first scientific account of the land of the Pharaohs. The whole subject, however, would have remained in the realm of conjecture had it not been for the discovery in 1799 by an artillery officer named Boussard, of the 'Rosetta Stone'. Thanks to this stone, Champollion succeeded, in 1822, in solving the mystery of hieroglyphic writing. From then onwards epigraphy and archaeology moved forward hand in hand to a systematic exploration of the Egyptian field.

Progress was slower in Mesopotamia. The region of the Tigris and the Euphrates contained no great groups of monuments like those of Egypt, but only heaps of ruins, for the most part unimposing, the haunt of jackals and panthers. Although it had been visited in 1172 by Benjamin of Tudela, Palmyra, in the heart of the Syrian desert, may be said to have been rediscovered by an Italian, Pietro della Valle (1616), and a Frenchman, Jean-Baptiste Tavernier (1630). Baalbek was visited, in 1757, by an English traveller, Robert Wood. But these two cities belonged visibly to later civilizations. They marked the period of Roman domination in Syria.

Thus, at the beginning of the nineteenth century nothing was known of the Assyrians beyond what was recorded in the Bible. Of the Sumerians, the Akkadians and the Hittites, nothing at all was known. In short, the historical map was but a large blank. At the very most, Babylon was correctly placed on the banks of the Euphrates, and Nineveh, somewhat hesitantly, on the east bank of the Tigris. In Europe the bas-reliefs, and still more the signs carved on the famous black stone, brought back in 1786 by Michaux, were the source of considerable perplexity.

The mystery of Mesopotamia was to defy solution longer than the Egyptian enigma. Nevertheless the attack was resumed, and more and more prospecting of the surface was carried out. British Residents bustled about over the country, in particular officials of the East India Company, like C. J. Rich, from 1807 to 1821, and

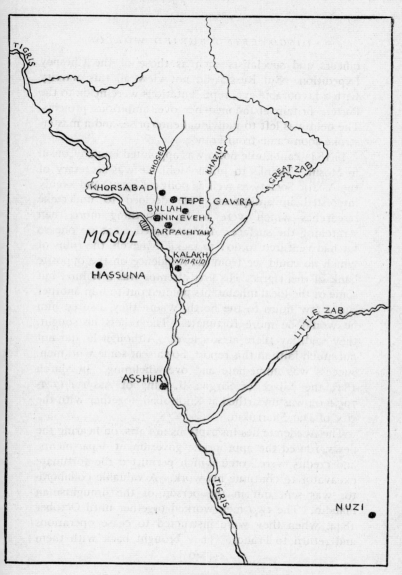

I. Assyria and the Upper Tigris

officers and specialists such as those of the Chesney Expedition. But Russia did not view all this activity with a favourable eye; representations were made to the Porte. Britain abandoned her over-ambitious projects. The field was left to individual enterprise, and a masterstroke soon came from France.

In 1842 Paul-Emile Botta was appointed French Consul in Mosul. Thanks to Julius Mohl, he was secretary of the Asiatic Society as well as political agent, and keenly interested in antiquities. He decided to undertake researches which were to be something more than scratching the surface. He attempted what no one so far had ventured to do : to tackle Nineveh, the ruins of which he could see from his Residence on the opposite bank of the Tigris. His first attempt was a failure, but some of the local inhabitants pointed out to him another site a few miles to the north, where they assured him he would be more fortunate. The reliefs he sought, they said, lay there at soil level. Although he did not put much faith in this report, Botta sent some workmen. Success was immediate and overwhelming. In March 1843 the palace of Sargon II, King of Assyria (721-705 B.C.) was unearthed at Khorsabad, together with the city of Dur Sharrukin.

The Académie des Inscriptions in Paris, on hearing the news, roused the appropriate government departments, and credits were voted which permitted the fortunate excavator to continue his work. A valuable collaborator was sent out in the person of the draughtsman Flandin. The two men worked together until October 1844, when they were instructed to cease operations and return to France. They brought back with them quantities of drawings and copies of inscriptions, while at Basra the *Cormoran* took on board the cases containing the antiquities. They were unloaded at Le Havre, and brought up the Seine, arriving in Paris in February 1847. On the first of May the first Assyrian room in Europe was inaugurated at the Louvre.

Nevertheless the civilization of Assyria could not be fully understood as long as its writing remained undeciphered. With the help of trilingual inscriptions copied in Persia, at Persepolis and Behistun, and using the mass of documents found at Khorsabad and at other sites on which digging had started, several scholars struggled towards success. In 1857 Rawlinson, Hincks and Oppert, all three translating simultaneously the same Assyrian text, showed that victory was assured.

Botta's successes mark the beginning of a long period of exploration which has been interrupted only by the two world wars. At various times all the great nations have taken part. In this often hotly fought contest, with its occasional dramatic moments, the British and French were for a long time the chief rivals. The Americans and Germans entered the field later, and spared no effort to equal the successes of those who had preceded them. Lastly the Departments of Antiquities of the new States, Syria and Iraq, came into action in their turn, and were soon obtaining excellent results.

Such a story is not easy to summarize. I shall, however, choose the most salient facts in this long saga of discovery—for that is what it is—an epic, moreover, which is still continuing before our eyes. We must return to Botta.

Britain at once understood the lesson of Khorsabad.

Hardly had Botta returned to France when Austen Henry Layard arrived in Mosul (1845). He set to work energetically on the great royal cities of Nineveh, Kalakh (Nimrud), and Asshur (Qal'at Sharqat), obtaining such convincing results that his mission was renewed (1849-1851). The sites were intact, and everywhere it was necessary for the excavator only to turn over the soil to reap a rich harvest. But in those days what was sought above all was the antique object, the museum-piece. The archaeological context was considered to be of little importance or interest.

Faced with these British successes France realized that through her absence opportunities were being missed. Two official expeditions were despatched to Mesopotamia; one under Victor Place was to continue Botta's work at Nineveh and Khorsabad, and the other, under Fresnel, was to excavate Babylon.

Victor Place completed (1852-1854) the excavation of Sargon's palace, the plan of which was drawn by the architect Thomas, winner of the Grand Prix de Rome. Further important reliefs were sent down the Tigris to be embarked at Basra. With them were crates sent by Fresnel, whose activities at Babylon had had only mediocre results. On 21st May 1855 the convoy was attacked at Qurna and the boats were sunk in the Tigris. With considerable difficulty a few items were salvaged, among which were one of the androcephalous bulls and the big winged genie, now in the Louvre (Plate 15). But several fine pieces were lost for ever. While Place, in the confusion that followed, pursued a troubled consular career, Fresnel died in penury at Baghdad in November 1855.

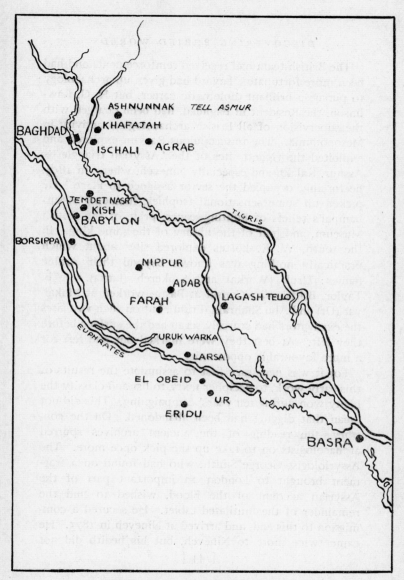

II. Central and Southern Mesopotamia

The British team had received reinforcements and had been more fortunate. Layard had given up archaeology to pursue a brilliant diplomatic career, but H. G. Rawlinson, the Resident in Baghdad, had been charged with the supervision of all British archaeological activity in Mesopotamia. The unscrupulous Rassam explored and exploited the richest sites of the ' Assyrian triangle '— Asshur, Kalakh and especially Nineveh, where, in 1853, he forcibly occupied the sector assigned to Place. He picked up some sensational trophies, including Assurbanipal's reliefs of hunting-scenes, pride of the British Museum, and half of the library of the same king. In the south, W. K. Loftus explored sites about which practically nothing was known beyond their Arabic names : Uruk (Warka) and Senkereh (Larsa). J. E. Taylor, British Vice-Consul at Basra, worked at Mukaiyar (Ur) and Abu Shahrain (Eridu), but on such vast sites the excavators had scarcely scratched the surface before they left. At best they were marked out and left for a more favourable opportunity.

For it was necessary first to assimilate the results of this early work, to decipher texts, to list and classify the booty won during ten years' campaigning. This did not mean that digging had been abandoned. On the contrary, the reading of the ancient archives spurred archaeologists on to take up the pick once more. The Assyriologist George Smith, who had found on a fragment brought to London an important part of the Assyrian account of the Flood, wished to find the remainder of the mutilated tablet. He secured a commission to this end, and arrived at Nineveh in 1873. He came twice more to Nineveh, but his health did not stand up to the rude oriental climate, and he died at Aleppo in 1876. This was the signal for the reappearance of Rassam, and the skimming and pillaging of the sites, to the great detriment of later scientific investigation.

France had been absent from the field for twenty years, but shortly afterwards she made a brilliant re-entry. She had not entirely abandoned the East, for, in 1860, the Semitic scholar, Ernest Renan, accompanying the expeditionary force sent by Napoleon III to the Levant after the massacres at Zahle and Deir el Qamar, carried out some digging on several Phoenician sites: Byblos, Sidon, Tyre, Umm el Awamid, Rowad and Amrit. Although he was in the area only from the 21st October 1860 to 24th September 1861 he brought back not only his *Life of Jesus* (1863), but also an abundance of documents which he published in *Mission de Phénicie* (1864), the first extensive account of Phoenician archaeology. Nevertheless, attention was soon to be directed towards Mesopotamia, where the Frenchman de Sarzec had renewed the great tradition.

Ernest de Sarzec, Vice-Consul at Basra, was one of those diplomats who had come under the spell of archaeology. At Tello, in 1877, he discovered the ancient city of Lagash, disclosing monuments of a hitherto unknown civilization which was to become known as Sumerian. The operations, approved by the French authorities and by Léon Heuzey, of the Institute, were conducted at first in the utmost secrecy, and continued officially until 1900. After directing eleven campaigns and collecting a considerable haul of antiquities, which were divided between the Louvre and the Imperial Ottoman Museum, de Sarzec had to give up his diplomatic and archaeological work on account of ill-health. He returned to France and died at Poitiers on 31st May, 1901. His successes brought rivals into the field, not only English, but also, for the first time, Germans and Americans.

The German architect, Dr. R. Koldewey, after a brief campaign at Surghul and El Hibbah (1887), two sites near Tello, turned his attention in 1899 to the exploration of Babylon, a work which was to continue for the next eighteen years until it was halted abruptly in 1917 by the vicissitudes of the First World War. The same expedition also excavated the Babylonian sites of Borsippa, Shuruppak (Fara) and Abu Hatab. It even went further afield and set to work in 1903 on the Assyrian royal city of Asshur, where Dr. Walter Andrae perfected in masterly fashion a new technique of excavation applicable to situations where the intermingling of the layers of architectural remains renders the task of identification and interpretation a complicated and hazardous one. Removing the strata on an archaeological site is never quite as simple as cutting off the layers of a sandwich cake.

The American archaeologists chose Nippur, whose ancient name survives in the Arabic Nuffar. They began digging in 1899, but serious differences of opinion within the expedition hindered the work. In 1900, after the fourth campaign, the site was closed, and, the controversies continuing, further excavation was postponed *sine die*. The work was not taken up again until 1948 with, of course, a new team.

Meanwhile the English, represented in Mesopotamia

from 1878 to 1882 by Rassam alone, continued the policy of remaining on the spot. From 1885 to 1890 Wallis Budge worked in Babylonia, but on the whole the British Museum remained faithful to Assyria and the northern region. In 1903, L. W. King opened up the excavations at Nineveh, while others prospected in the region of the Upper Euphrates. The Hittite city of Carchemish was chosen, and a carefully composed expedition began work there in 1911. At the same time Max Freiherr von Oppenheim, who knew northern Syria well, decided to excavate Tell Halaf, a town near the source of the Khabur River, close to the route surveyed in preparation for the construction of the railway to Baghdad.

While the English and Germans occupied positions as favourable to archaeology as to diplomacy, the French seem to have forsaken Assyria altogether. They were attracted rather by the land of Sumer, where, at Tello in 1903, Captain G. Cros took up the work where de Sarzec had left it. He remained there until 1909, when his military duties compelled him to give up archaeology. In 1912 the Abbé H. de Genouillac was granted a concession for work at Kish, another royal city near Babylon, while on the marches of the Iranian plateau J. de Morgan continued on an ever vaster scale the excavation of Susa, begun in 1897 following two fruitful campaigns that had been conducted there (1884-1886) by Jane and Marcel Dieulafoy.

In Europe work continued unabated on the daily more numerous documents that poured from the sites. First the Assyrians, then the Sumerians, and now the Hittites, were brought back into the field of history. The

Assyrian tongue had surrendered all its secrets; that of the Sumerians had few of its secrets left once Thureau-Dangin had successfully analysed its mechanism. But the deciphering of Sumerian writings had scarcely begun when the explosion of the First World War marked the end of an epoch in archaeological investigation.

*　　*　　*

The armistice signed on 30th October 1918 at Mudros had marked the cessation of hostilities in the Middle East. Shortly afterwards Iraq and Syria had come under British and French mandate respectively. Certain zones previously considered dangerous were becoming more accessible. In them archaeologists would now be able to carry out prolonged researches. Whereas until then the world of archaeology had remained on the margin of official preoccupations, now Departments of Antiquities were formed in the various regions, which took steps to make a census of the sites and assure their preservation and custody. Clandestine enterprises were brought to an end, digging being carefully controlled to ensure its efficacy.

New opportunities were presenting themselves, but the necessary qualified personnel was lacking. So far, use had been made of the help of diplomats, army officers, engineers or Assyriologists. The time had come to train archaeologists. The School of Athens and the French Institute in Cairo were sending men to the archaeological sites of Greece and Egypt. Nothing similar existed for Syria or for Mesopotamia. A French archaeological school was therefore founded in Jerusalem, near the monastery of the Dominicans from the Biblical School. Every year the Académie des Inscriptions et Belles-Lettres sent out a student, who was frequently chosen from among those graduating from the Ecole du Louvre.

Between the wars the whole of the Middle East was subjected to intensive exploration. It is probable that with the passage of time the years 1919-1939 will come to be looked upon as the Golden Age of oriental archaeology.

The British, first in the field, to begin with had Mesopotamia to themselves. Indeed, Iraq was under British mandate, and the excavators from the British Museum had the benefit of all the support they could wish. Campbell Thompson (1918), then H. R. Hall (1919) and lastly Sir Leonard Woolley (1922), chose the district of Ur. Neither Taylor nor Loftus had completely despoiled it, and the most important remains were still to be discovered. Hall dug a new site, Obeid, revealing a richly decorated temple with a wealth of votive offerings. Meanwhile, Woolley was carrying out the systematic exploration of Ur which was long over-due. The work took twelve years to complete, and was marked by a series of sensational discoveries, among which was that of the 'royal tombs' (1927-1929), whose treasures rivalled those of Tutankhamen which Howard Carter had only recently uncovered in the Valley of the Kings (1922-1924).

About the same time an Anglo-American expedition established itself at Kish, not far from Babylon. Under the direction of Professor S. Langdon of Oxford, the expedition doubtless looked for fruitful results in the royal city (four dynasties of Kish are mentioned in the king-lists). Although ten years of sustained effort (1923-1933) produced little in the way of museum-pieces, the scientific results were important, for on the nearby site of Jamdat Nasr the expedition found remains which were recognized as a further phase of that Mesopotamian proto-history one stage of which had already been revealed by the Obeid excavations.

A third phase was shortly to come to light following the methodical excavation of Warka, the Sumerian town of Uruk (Erech of Gen. 10.10). The German archaeologists, who had begun digging there in 1913, returned in 1928. All of them trained architects, the various leaders (Jordan, Nöldeke, Heinrich) were interested first and foremost in architecture, meticulously clearing and detailing each item as one might with pieces of marquetry. One result of these scrupulous methods was a clearer appreciation of the superposition of the strata which, starting from virgin soil and ending with the surface ruins, represent all the phases of occupation. With the lowest stratum we are not far from the fifth millennium B.C.; at the top we are almost into the Christian era.

At last it was the turn of the French. They came back to Tello in 1929. Their delay is easily explained. Since 1919 French effort had been concentrated on Syria and the Lebanon. These territories had been mandated to France by the League of Nations, and it was there that effective material support for French archaeologists was most readily forthcoming. She had not wasted her time there. At Byblos, Pierre Montet, looking for traces of Egyptian activity, discovered as early as 1921 the

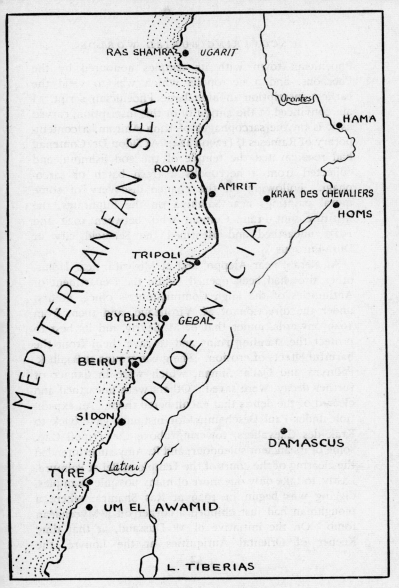

III. *Phoenicia*

Phoenician town with its temples honoured by the Pharaohs, and a necropolis which was to yield the earliest inscription in alphabetic Phoenician script. I am convinced of the antiquity of this inscription, carved as it is on the sarcophagus of King Ahiram, a contemporary of Rameses II (1290-1224). At Sidon Dr. Contenau had re-excavated the temple of the god Eshmun, and collected from a necropolis a fresh batch of sarcophagi. Following on the chance discovery of some mural paintings near Salahiya on the Euphrates, the Institute sent Franz Cumont who, between 1922 and 1925, unearthed and identified the Seleucid city of Dura-Europus.

At Nerab, near Aleppo, and at Mishrifa, near Homs, other sites had been opened, while the Department of Antiquities of the High Commissioner's office, at first under the direction of M. Virolleaud, and then, from 1929 onwards, under that of M. Seyrig, did its best to protect the standing ruins and to save them from the harmful effects of erosion. The great groups at Baalbek, Palmyra and Qal'at Siman, which were in danger of further decay, were saved. Others were unearthed and cleared of the debris that encumbered them. An expedition under Paul Deschamps, for instance, gave back to Krak des Chevaliers, towering above the Tripoli Gap, some of its ancient splendour; and R. Amy superintended the clearing of the court of the Temple of Bel at Palmyra. Lastly, to take only one more of many possible examples, digging was begun in 1929 at Ras Shamra, where a ploughman had just chipped a corner off a Mycenaean tomb. On the initiative of M. Dussaud, at that time Keeper of Oriental Antiquities at the Louvre, the

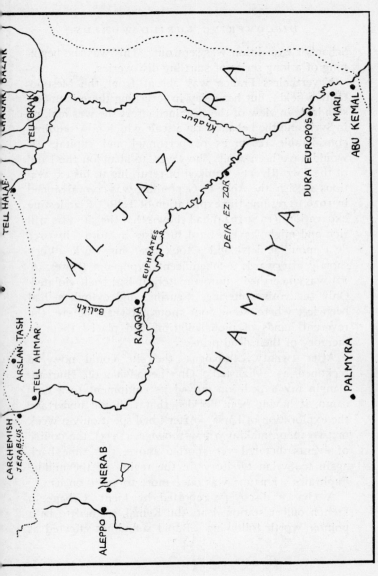

IV. Middle Euphrates, Khabur and Upper Euphrates

Schaeffer expedition was sent out. This was the beginning of a long series of startling discoveries.

Nevertheless France was absent from the Mesopotamian field. But her delay in returning there is understandable in view of the sustained effort she was making in Syria and the Lebanon, on a scale which now required considerable resources of personnel and capital. It would have been a pity, however, to abandon the Land of the Two Rivers. Baulked of returning to his excavations at Kish, the Abbé de Genouillac was commissioned in 1929 to resume the exploration of Tello. Clandestine excavations (1923-1924) had shown that the site was still rich and might have several surprises in store. In 1931 de Genouillac left, and I took over his work. Very shortly afterwards a magnificent hypogeum (Plates 16, 17) was unearthed—unfortunately it had been violated. Only the votive offerings (figurines and cylinders) had been left where, some four thousand years before, the reverent hands of pious pilgrims had placed them in memory of their dead princes.

After twenty campaigns, the site could now be reckoned as exhausted. On the advice of Thureau-Dangin my expedition moved its equipment to a new camp, it having been decided that I should undertake the exploration of Larsa. After I had spent only a week or two there, making a few *sondages* (1933), the course of events dictated yet another move, this time back again to Syrian territory, in the region of the middle Euphrates. Fortune was once more to smile on us.

A chance discovery reported by Lieut. Cabane, a French officer stationed at Abu Kemal, seemed to be a pointer worth following. Rapid soundings effected at

Tell Hariri in the autumn of 1933 confirmed the impression which had led M. Dussaud to request permission for me to dig there. In January 1934 the discovery of a temple with inscribed votive offerings enabled me to identify the *tell* as another capital of the Babylonian world, the royal city of Mari. I went back every year until 1939, when operations were suspended because of the war. In November 1951 it became possible to resume the work, which still continues.

Meanwhile other expeditions had continued working in the area of the middle Euphrates, and new ones had been attracted to it. A few miles upstream from Mari the excavation of Dura-Europus, begun, as I have already said, by Franz Cumont, had been resumed in 1928 by the University of Yale in association with the Académie des Inscriptions et Belles-Lettres. It was to continue until 1937. It was also in 1928 that François Thureau-Dangin began work on Arslan Tash in Upper Syria, and then, in 1929, on Tell Ahmar. In both places he uncovered Assyrian cities, bringing back from the former site a magnificent collection of ivories, which may be seen to-day in the Louvre and in the Aleppo Museum.

The valley of the Khabur, a tributary of the Euphrates, was thoroughly prospected by the English archaeologist M. E. L. Mallowan, one of the foremost authorities on oriental ceramics. He had visited more than a hundred *tells*, choosing two for methodical excavation, when in 1939 the war came to interrupt fruitful researches.

*　　　*　　　*

But we must come back to the region of the upper

Tigris, which had been the subject of most careful study by expeditions which with one exception (that of the Italians to Kakzu) were all Anglo-Saxon. In archaeology there appears to be a sort of tacit agreement that the efforts of the organizations of the various nations should not overlap. One of the most powerful expeditions that was ever in the field was that sponsored by the Oriental Institute of Chicago, which owed its creation to Rockefeller, and which was at that time under the direction of J. H. Breasted. Having at its disposal practically unlimited capital, and resources on the scale of the industrial potential of the New World, the Oriental Institute had set itself, among others, the task of excavating systematically at carefully selected points along the 'Fertile Crescent', from the Iranian plateau to Upper Egypt. These points had been chosen for varying reasons. Some of them were places renowned in history and therefore likely to be fruitful of results (e.g. Luxor in Egypt, Megiddo in Palestine, Khorsabad in Assyria, Persepolis in Iran). Others were sites which had become famous owing to the chance discovery of ancient monuments (e.g. Tainat in Upper Syria) or through clandestine operations (e.g. Tell Asmar and Khafajah in Iraq). It was decided that the time had come to send out an expedition.

The largest and best equipped was the Iraq Expedition. Magnificently, even luxuriously, established not far from Baghdad, at Tell Asmar, it worked on several sites, beginning in 1930. Under Dr. Henri Frankfort, digging was carried out either simultaneously or successively at Asmar, Khafajah, Ajrab and Ischali, in the Diyala district. At each place important discoveries were made, and from the ancient temples a very fine collection of antique statuary was assembled.

The Iraq Expedition had also requested a concession at Khorsabad, the site of previous work by the Frenchmen Botta and Place. But even with their rich resources and improved techniques the Americans could scarcely hope to eclipse the results obtained by these French excavators. A palace shorn of its reliefs a century ago cannot produce new ones now! Nevertheless a few pieces did remain, for Botta and Place, limited in their choice, had been unable to remove them. The Oriental Institute was thus able to pick up a few important gleanings left over from the earlier harvest. It was in the sectors that had remained intact that the excavators had their due reward.

Possessing fewer resources, but just as sure in their methods, other American organizations had turned their attention to less extensive ruins or more modest *tells*. But in archaeology there is no 'greater' or 'lesser'. Every result is valuable, and it is not necessarily the smallest sites which have least to say in this great retelling of the story of the past.

At Nuzi, not far from the Kirkuk oilfields, then at Tepe Gawra, and finally at Tell Billah, the American School of Oriental Research, one of the most energetic organizations in this field, undertook excavations conducted with faultless technique by numerous highly skilled archaeologists, among whom were Chiera, Pfeiffer, Starr, Bache and Delougaz, to mention but a few.

In each case the operations were carried out, from the surface levels downwards, in such a manner that the superposition of successive civilizations was clearly revealed, and their essential characteristics, their common or distinctive features, could be noted. Slowly the great eras of Mesopotamian proto-history were reconstituted. One after another the blanks were filled in. Relative dating with neighbouring civilizations was made possible, disclosing thus their relationship and their mutual influence throughout the long process of human development.

The British were also at work in the upper Tigris. They still remained faithful to Nineveh, but since the time of Layard, perspectives had widened. When, in 1927, Campbell Thompson set up camp again there, he was determined not to restrict himself to the Assyrian period—a century ago no one imagined that there was any other—but to dig down towards the origins of civilization. Thus did the Assyrian capital reveal, one by one, the periods of its past. And indeed they were found to correspond with what was anticipated in the light of discoveries made independently by the Americans in neighbouring excavations. Still further confirmation was forthcoming in 1933 when Mallowan, exploring the mound of Arpachiyah, three and a half miles from Nineveh, discovered that it contained, superimposed one upon another, fifteen levels of an entirely archaic civilization. The imagination falters when one considers how much of the past lay enclosed in those thin leaves of earth.

So it was that everywhere horizontal exploration was accompanied now by vertical excavation. The expeditions at work on the various sites vied with one another in producing, year by year, more and better stratigraphical sections. At the same time the area under research was increasing, as their investigations led the archaeologists farther and farther afield. When one has picked up a thread it is natural to wish to follow it to its end, in time as well as in space. 'Painted' pottery, for example, from the moment it was recognized as affording a valuable criterion, became one of these threads. Starting from the Phoenician coast or from the Anatolian plateaux, the archaeologists had perforce to look successively, beyond Mesopotamia, beyond Susiana, towards the vast expanse of Persia, to the Caspian, to Afghanistan, Baluchistan, and the Indus valley. Some even directed their gaze farther still, towards distant China.

At the same time, the wider the horizons that must be included in one's view, the more necessary it becomes to make a thorough study of a few limited sectors. There is no other way of progressing in a science whose complexity has increased considerably during the last twenty years. The days seem to have gone when a Georges Perrot could handle, with equal sureness of touch, the art of the Ramessids, the style of Phidias and the Assyrian colossi. In the domain of the history of art only André Malraux is able to master the whole enormous mass of the subject, discerning at once what must be set apart as being of special significance. But in archaeology it is difficult now to unravel at once and with equal felicity the Hyksos enigma, the Sumerian problem, and the puzzle of the writings of ancient India. These are tasks which must be undertaken by different men. Working side by side in each sector are the archaeologist, the epigraphist and the architect, for it is seldom, not to say never, possible for one man to retain in his hands and mind the vast amount of relevant documentary material that has come to light.

*　　　*　　　*

Naturally, the Second World War slowed down archaeological research considerably. For the most part, the expedition leaders were either mobilized or unable to leave the countries of Europe or the New World. In any case the great nations, occupied in the conduct of the war, would not have been able adequately to finance expensive operations. It was necessary to wait for the return of happier days when the wounds of war had healed. The young explorers of the inter-war years had all grown old. However, when the Departments of Antiquities of the newly created States, Iraq and Syria in particular, did grant them the necessary authorization, almost to a man they were able to return. M. E. L. Mallowan took up again the exploration of Nimrud, begun by Layard, and the sensational discoveries made there in 1952 showed that the site was not yet exhausted; C. F. A. Schaeffer went back to Ras Shamra; I myself was able to pick up the threads again at Mari. A new American team was installed at Nippur, continuing the tradition of Peters and Haynes, while the veteran Sir Leonard Woolley was able to complete his excavations at Atchana.

In their turn Iraqi and Syrian archaeologists came into action. Prompted by Dr. Naji el Asil, the Department of Antiquities of Iraq undertook digging at Hassuna, Eridu, Tell 'Uqair and Hatra. Notable success has been achieved by Fuad Safar and Taha Baqir. Hatra produced, in 1951 and 1952, some extraordinary examples of Parthian sculpture. In Syria, following the Emir Jafar, Dr. Selim Abdulhak has devoted himself entirely to the heavy task of preserving, restoring and excavating the ancient sites of a country rich in history. In the Lebanon the same task has been undertaken by the Emir Maurice Chehab, while M. Dunand has continued the excavation of Byblos.

I have purposely confined myself in this rapid sketch to the eastern arm of the Fertile Crescent. I hope it will suffice to give the reader some idea not only of the labours accomplished in the last hundred years, but also of the great scientific activity of which the Middle East has for a century been the chosen field. I might have dwelt more on other regions—the Iranian plateau (Susa, where R. Ghirshman is following in the steps of the Dieulafoys, de Morgan and Mecquenem), Anatolia (where the limelight has suddenly been concentrated on Haran and Karatepe), Israel and Jordan (who has not heard of the Dead Sea Scrolls?), and lastly Egypt (with Tanis, where Pierre Montet has continued the successes he achieved at Byblos).

I have confined myself to one region, but all the other sectors tell the same story. Everywhere archaeologists have rolled back the past, or, at least, the veil which hid it from a knowledge ever more thorough and ever more eager to learn. For man is not content to remain in ignorance; and as his mind is always on the alert, and since, among his great problems, that of the origins of civilization is one of those that attract him most, it was inevitable that modern research should come to be centred upon the land to which every tradition, secular or sacred, traced the cradle of humanity, locating in it one of the crucibles of civilization.

So far I have attempted to show how men set about disengaging the past from its shroud of earth. I have quoted the names of a few of the artisans engaged in that task, which belongs not to one single nation, but to the whole thinking world as it reflects upon its origins. The time has come now to pass to a reckoning of the heritage that has been reconquered.

III

FIVE THOUSAND YEARS
OF CIVILIZATION

ONCE AGAIN we must limit ourselves to one region and
treat it in broad outline. First of all let us define the
province of art and civilization to which we shall be
confined.

Geographically, it extends from the Mediterranean in
the west to the Iranian plateau in the east, from Anatolia in the north to the Sinai desert in the south.

The chronological limits are simple to state. The first
lie at the origins of civilization, well into the fifth millennium B.C., and the last are at the beginning of the
Christian era.

Ethnographically the problem is infinitely more complex, for we are faced with different races, different
peoples, in each sector: Sumerians in lower Mesopotamia; Akkadians in central Mesopotamia; Assyrians in
Assyria; Elamites and Achaemenid Persians in Persia;
Hurrites between the upper Tigris and Euphrates; Hittites
in Anatolia; Phoenicians on the Mediterranean coast;
Canaanites in Palestine; Aramaean Syrians in the plains
of the interior. From the time of Alexander the Great
and his meteoric passage across the eastern world,
foreign populations are superimposed upon the ancient
indigenous stock, so that thereafter we find Greeks,
Romans, and then Parthians.

[63]

This list alone—very much simplified though it is—suffices to show that civilization did not develop in western Asia with that fundamental unity which we find in Egypt, but that on the contrary it was the work of various peoples. It follows that there is not *one* civilization of ancient western Asia, nor, therefore, *one* art, but several civilizations and several arts, marked by each race with its own peculiar imprint, its inspiration—in a word, its genius. From this it follows also that in cultural development each region played its part. Out of the labour of all, and through the synthesis of the efforts of all, civilization was forged.

In this great achievement two peoples stand out clearly, surpassing all the rest: the Mesopotamians in the east and the Phoenicians in the west. On the one hand are great empires, extending their hegemony to the distant limits set by natural barriers, for it is the impassable line that makes the only real frontier; on the other is a little nation, its back to the land, its gaze ever fixed upon the sea. Born sailors and navigators no doubt they were, but one inspired invention has made them immortal: the alphabet. While every other nation had required several hundred signs with which to express its thoughts and give visible form to human speech, the Phoenicians invented twenty-two signs which, easy to distinguish and simple to execute, covered perfectly every sound in the language.

Compared with these two aspects of human achievement—the highly developed, even refined, civilization of Mesopotamia, and the invention of the alphabet in Phoenicia—Palestine, a poor and disinherited land, lacking in mineral wealth, added nothing in these domains

1. The *tell* of Khan Sheikhun (Syria)

2. Senkereh-Larsa (Iraq)

3. Horned viper killed in the excavations at Mari

4. Tell Hariri before the excavations (1933)

5. Tell Hariri-Mari after four seasons' digging

6. Mari: Alabaster head on the step of a staircase
(Aleppo Museum)

7. Mari: Statue of the governor Ishtup-ilum, *in situ*

8. Mari: The governor Ishtup-ilum (nineteenth century B.C.)
(Aleppo Museum)

9. Mari: An Assyrian tomb after excavation (eleventh century B.C.)

10. Tello-Lagash: Tombs of the Gudea period (twenty-second century B.C.)

11. Mari: Statuettes from the temple of Ishtar
(first half of the third millennium B.C.)

12. Mari: Statuettes from the temple of Ishtar
(first half of the third millennium B.C.)

13. Tello: Start of the stratigraphical excavation

14. Tello: Progress of the stratigraphical excavation

KHORSABAD Palais du roi SARGON VIII Siècle.

15. Khorsabad: Winged genie (eighth century B.C.) (Louvre)

16. Tello: 'Hypogeum of the *patesis*' from the south

17. Tello: 'Hypogeum of the *patesis*' from the west

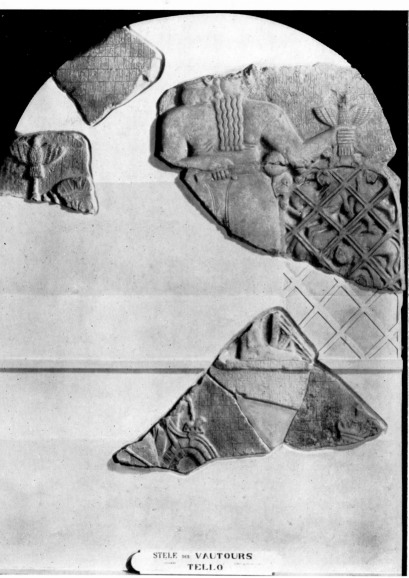

STELE DES VAUTOURS
TELLO

18. Tello: Stele of the Vultures (twenty-seventh century B.C.)
(Louvre)

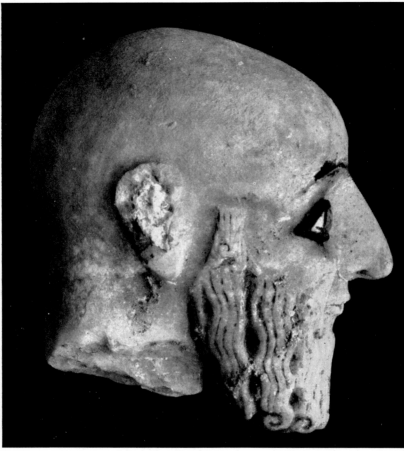

19. Mari: Ebih-il, the steward (twenty-seventh century B.C.)
(Louvre)

20. Stele of Naram-Sin (twenty-fourth century B.C.)
(Louvre)

21. Nineveh: King Assurbanipal (Louvre)

22. Susa: Achaemenid capital from the palace of Artaxerxes
(405–362 B.C.) (Louvre)

23. Malatya: Hittite bas-relief of a stag-hunt
(tenth–ninth centuries B.C.) (Louvre)

24. Lion from Sheikh Saad (tenth–ninth centuries B.C.)
(Damascus Museum)

25. Tyre: The harbour in 1930

26. Byblos: The ancient harbour in 1928

27. Baalbek: The so-called 'Temple of Bacchus'
(second–third centuries A.D.)

28. Palmyra: A general view of the ruins

29. Bronze Sursock Heliopolitan Jupiter
(second–third centuries A.D.) (Louvre)

30. Petra: Funerary temple called *El Khazna* (The Treasure)
(photograph by the author)

that was not borrowed from elsewhere. But her soil is sacred, for the believers of three monotheistic world-religions have their holy places there. Nineveh and Babylon are no more than ruined wastes or heaps of rubble, Tyre is shorn of all its former splendour. In spite of all the storms of time Jerusalem has survived, and for Jews, Christians and Moslems it remains their City.

*   *   *

Etymologically, Mesopotamia is the land between the two rivers, Euphrates and Tigris. A vast level plain, formed mainly of alluvium, sun, soil and water together ensure its fertility. The traveller, arriving among the palm-groves of this plain, encased and emphasized in a rocky ring of desert and plateau, is reminded of the garden planted in Eden.

It is not surprising that from the earliest times civilization discerned and found there a home where it might flourish. Both Sumerians and Semites brought to that civilization the tribute of their race and their inventive spirit.

However, they met two major obstacles: the lack of stone and the absence of mineral deposits. Hence the necessity of having a different type of architecture, using the natural resources of the land, namely clay and reeds, and the inescapable obligation of importing metal.

Doubtless it is this permanent struggle which lies behind the affirmation of force as a sign of power. But into this force the Semites were to introduce a touch of finesse, of delicate sensibility. The Sumerian is always

C

grave; the Semite knows how to smile. The fantasy of the one is superimposed on the hieratic conventionalism of the other. Mesopotamian civilization is made up of their harmony and their contrasts.

Though this was true of the early periods, it was not maintained, for with the Assyrians, an exclusively Semitic people, all, or almost all, the joy seems to have disappeared. Theirs was the era of stern implacable Mars, an age of war, nothing but war, and always war, for the hunt is but a training for the battle-field. It was time for the Achaemenid peace to bring its balm to torn humanity. But this proved to be no more than an interlude in preparation for the arrival of Alexander of Macedonia and the triumph of Hellenism.

*　　　*　　　*

I must here define more precisely the sequence of these different phases of Mesopotamian civilization, illustrating them by means of some of their sculptured monuments.

Up to the time of the Second World War three stages were distinguished in the proto-history of Mesopotamia. These were named after the three sites on which they were first discovered and their differing features recognized. Thus, starting from the origins, one passed through the periods of Obeid, Uruk and Jamdat Nasr, arriving in the period of history about the year 3000 B.C.

It is now known that the Obeid phase was preceded by several others, at least four of which have been defined, being given the names of Hassuna, Samarra, Halaf and Eridu. It is true that the Samarra and Halaf cultures were known before 1939, but they were thought to be of later date, parallel with the Obeid period. These new names correspond to four clearly defined stages whose sequence is now established beyond any possible doubt. This journey backwards in time takes us well into the fifth millennium B.C. Step by step we are approaching the threshold of pre-history with its caves. The earliest village of all found so far, older than Hassuna, is that of Jarmo, in northern Iraq, which represents the first rural habitation in the open air, with houses and tools but as yet without pottery. This particular stage of civilization could therefore be described as 'pre-ceramic'. Nevertheless these men, who had not yet realized that they could shape clay so as to make vessels, were already modelling it into figurines. In these little models of animals and of women we see the first glimmerings of a spiritual life, the first attempts at representation, the beginnings of art.

It is not possible within the framework of a rapid sketch to describe in detail each one of these great periods. But I shall try to give an indication of their character by describing some of their distinctive features.

While the people of the Hassuna period show themselves, from the beginning of the fifth millennium B.C., to have been conscientious craftsmen, already taking the trouble to decorate their everyday vessels, those of the Samarra and Halaf cultures made an important advance: the conquest of metal. With the use of copper in the manufacture of tools and weapons—previously made only of wood, stone, clay or bone—men were entering an age of upheaval, for progress always entails radical modifications in social structure. The era of the village-agglomeration was giving way to that of the city-agglomeration. The concentration of previously isolated dwellings brought in its train new architectural achievements: public and religious buildings, and royal residences. This evolution continued in a way that is remarkable when we bear in mind that every fresh development was an innovation, a new creation.

The spirit of invention was given free rein. Although writing has not yet been discovered, it is certain that here and there thought is expressed, particularly in the pottery, whose ornamentation is a veritable language. It would be rash to claim that the key to it has been found, or that the combinations of markings have all an obvious significance. But it would be difficult to doubt the symbolic value of the bucrane, the swastika, the double axe and the Maltese cross, already found in the fifth millennium B.C., and reproduced in the same forms in the mid-twentieth century A.D. by national and popular leaders, whose imaginations had been unable to devise anything other than these oriental themes!

It is obvious, given the alluvial character of the Mesopotamian basin, and its constant encroachment on the waters of the Persian Gulf, that the most ancient human vestiges must be sought in northern Iraq. Hassuna, Samarra and Halaf, the last near the head waters of the Khabur, are all in the upper region. In this civilization it is difficult to disentangle what is the product of the original inhabitants from what comes from elsewhere, for example from Persia, or even from further east.

It is indeed certain that Mesopotamia was a coveted land, and that aspirants to possess it might come from anywhere; anywhere, that is, where the land was poorer, less fertile—less like Paradise, in fact. For this reason incursions took place, many of them from the east. Evidence of one of them has recently been discovered, this time in southern Mesopotamia, in the lower strata of the city of Eridu.

Digging carried out by the Iraqi Department of Antiquities from 1946 to 1949 revealed an impressive superposition of dwellings in which those that were contemporary with Obeid were preceded by others that were so homogeneous, and yet so distinctive, that the majority of archaeologists now assign them to an 'Eridu' culture.

As regards architecture, there was found in the very earliest levels a sanctuary complete in all essential particulars. An offertory table, an altar, and a small chapel—nothing was lacking in this enclosure dedicated to worship and sacrifice.

As for ceramics, a beautifully shaped and richly decorated vessel was found, exclusively geometric in inspiration, as if the craftsmen had put away all idea of representation, devoting themselves entirely to abstract art.

Hassuna, Samarra, Halaf, Eridu : these are the stages that have been passed through, the blanks that archaeology has been able to fill in and define during the last ten years. The reader will understand now how progress has been speeded up with regard to the succeeding phases.

* * *

Obeid is a tiny *tell* a few miles from Ur. It gave its

name, in 1919, to a period of proto-history whose essential characteristics in the south were a type of pottery with a painted decoration, tools of stone or clay —it was most surprising to come upon sickles of the latter material—and strange figurines in the shape of men and women. The latter in particular, represented nude, have a decoration consisting of small attached lumps of clay, or touches of paint. Some of them bear a child in their arms, but the inexplicable thing about them is the snake-like face, surmounted by a head-dress of bitumen. What are we to make of this diminutive statuary? Are they real persons, whose faces the craftsman did not dare to portray? Or are they demons? The problem is still in dispute. In any case, these figurines are quite different from the statuettes of the Halaf period found in considerable numbers on many of the northern sites, which represent a woman in a sitting or crouching position, an attitude still adopted during parturition among certain Bedouin tribes.

The Obeid period also saw remarkable architectural development. Excavations at Gawra, near Nineveh, have revealed temples built in a style which bears witness to a bold inspiration and a proven technique. Discoveries of a like nature have been made at Eridu, which yielded the first example of a special type of temple, built on a high platform. This was the beginning of a tradition which was to be maintained through several millennia. The *ziggurat*, or staged tower, represents its final elaboration, being in essence a series of superimposed terraces, the last of which supports the sanctuary.

*　　　*　　　*

The two periods of Uruk and Jamdat Nasr, which follow, are characterized by fresh progress but also by profound upheavals. The Obeid culture, which had been imposed from the north upon the south of Mesopotamia, was clearly arrested in its evolution. The change can be attributed to the arrival of a new population, which may well be identified with the Sumerians.

From then on we see an extraordinary ferment in the most varied fields : architecture, sculpture, carving and metal work. The town of Uruk, in the middle of the fourth millennium B.C., must have been one of the most famous cities of Mesopotamia, on account of the splendour of its temples. There was no stone. Nothing daunted, its builders used sun-dried bricks, even having the audacity to set up clay columns. Massive, perhaps, they are, but the first essential was that they should be solid. But this did not mean that art was sacrificed. A type of mosaic was invented, consisting of terra-cotta cones inserted so that their bases showed on the surface, painted black, red and white. Façades and columns embellished in this way looked as if they were decked in immense multicoloured draperies.

And what of the sculpture? The first attempts are, of course, clumsy—the working of stone, an imported material, had to be learned from the beginning—but the craftsmen soon become artists. After the 'stele of the hunt', in which hunter and beasts are treated in broad outline, comes the delicacy of the alabaster temple vase, a marvel of light and line. The stratification of the remains has made it possible to determine the chronology of the events depicted. One can almost hear the tramp of the porters who come in procession to offer to the goddess Innin the finest fruits and vegetables and the choicest beasts from the herd.

As for the female mask also found at Uruk, it reveals with its expression of aristocratic sadness a sensitivity and sureness of execution which make it one of the most remarkable pieces not only of archaic sculpture, but of the sculpture of all time.

The last achievement was writing. Man discovered how to set down and transmit his speech. This, of course, did not mean that the oral message was abandoned. But the discovery was to set up a long chain reaction which no one can stop even now. Doubtless the system was still very complicated. It required several hundred signs, the learning and handling of which was a profession in itself. At this early stage drawings of objects—animals, plants, monuments, parts of the body—were used to represent things, if not sounds.

Behind this discovery we once more find the Sumerians. It is easier to say what the Sumerians were not than what they were. Neither Semitic nor Aryan. they outshone all the rest in creative genius and energy. By this time they controlled the whole of the south, the region which was henceforth to be called Sumer. Indirectly, through their civilization having imposed itself on them, they also controlled their immediate neighbours, the people of the Diyala; that is to say the inhabitants of the district where the two rivers Tigris and Euphrates approach one another as if they were about to join. But the renown of Sumer spread much farther north, its traditions inspiring the peoples of the middle Euphrates and the Khabur, as well as the upper Tigris.

We have reached the era of the great dynasties, which gave the supremacy first to one city and then to another. Henceforth we hear of Ur, of Kish, of Mari and again of Uruk. Their names are recorded in the king-lists, and excavations have demonstrated that they are not mistaken. What is less easy to understand is the absence from these lists of any mention of another great Sumerian metropolis, Lagash, whose glory was unequalled and whose *patesis* were among the most powerful of their day.

* * *

With the advent of writing, and the records of the names of cities and kings, we come to history, the threshold of which lies at the beginning of the third millennium B.C. This is the beginning of the great Sumerian phase, which we call 'pre-sargonic' (because it preceded the dynasty of Sargon of Agade) or the period of the 'first *patesis*'. British and American archaeologists know it by the name of 'early dynastic'. It covers the period from the twenty-ninth to the twenty-fifth centuries B.C.

The 'first *patesis*' often united in their persons the varied functions of political chief, general of the army, high priest, and grand master of the clergy. On the smooth running of public affairs and the judicious balance of commerce depended the ease and prosperity of the life of the 'royal' city. The *patesi* lived among his subjects as their guardian and patron. By his commands they lived, and by his directives the tone of their lives was set. There was work for all, whether architects, sculptors, metallurgists or goldsmiths. Their art drew its inspiration primarily from religion, which governed the whole of earthly life. Other artistic themes were furnished by military events.

At Lagash (the modern Tello), King Ur-Nanshe takes part with his sons in the laying of the first brick of the temple, the ceremony being followed by a sacred banquet. On a great stele, decorated on both sides (Plate 18), one of his successors, Eannatum, proudly commemorates the victory won with the help of the god Ningirsu over his bad neighbours of Umma. And always, everywhere, kings, governors, dignitaries, men and women commission or buy the little statues in soft stone—usually gypsum—which portray them in the ritual attitude of adoration, and which are to be placed on the sanctuary ledges.

There were workshops that specialized in the mass-production of these sculptures. Others were executed by artists who must have been famous in their day, although to us they remain anonymous, since they did not sign their works. No doubt these men copied the physiognomy of those for whom they worked. Thus we certainly possess the portraits of Ebih-il the steward (Plate 19), King Lamgi-Mari, and Idi-Narum the miller, all three of Mari, found in 1934 among the ruins of the temple of Ishtar.

In these statuettes from Mari, and in those from Lagash, Ashnunnak, Khafajah and Ajrab, we look once more on the faces, some smiling, others enigmatic, of the men and women of the beginning of the third millennium B.C. A strange look haunts their eyes, often still inlaid with shell and lapis lazuli, as if from beyond the tomb all these long-vanished people wished to reveal to us their secrets.

There are indeed many secrets from which the archaeologists have not yet succeeded in drawing back the veil. The most impressive and at the same time the most terrible of them is doubtless the mystery of the 'royal tombs' of Ur. What strange rites were these in which certain great personages of the Sumerian city— that they were of royal rank is by no means certain— were buried with all their treasures, and accompanied to the beyond by a whole retinue of courtiers and servants? About them lie warriors with their arms, charioteers with their vehicles and the animals that had drawn them still in harness, singing-girls and female attendants in their ceremonial costume.

Did all these people—in tomb No. 1237 as many as seventy-four, sixty-eight of them women, were counted —go down of their own free will into the sepulchres of their lords and masters, or were they compelled to accompany them into the life beyond the grave? Or is this perhaps the grim evidence of pitiless sacrifices, having regard to the quality and number of the victims, in connection with a fertility-cult, the fecundity of the land being secured at the cost of this mass immolation? Numerous hypotheses have been put forward to account for these hecatombs, and for the accumulation of so many precious objects around a single corpse. Recently the German orientalist Anton Moortgat has suggested that these burials, and the supposed violation of certain tombs, are connected with beliefs according to which Tammuz, the god who dies and is resurrected, was one of the principal deities of the Mesopotamian pantheon.

If the religious historian is left in the dark, not so the student of the history of art. He cannot fail to be impressed by the magnificence and the technical mastery revealed here by objects which may still to-day be counted as treasures. The rich glitter of yellow metal proclaims the prosperity of the Sumerian age. Here, at the beginning of the third millennium B.C., the high peaks of human achievement had been already scaled. Recent progress in our knowledge of proto-history makes the rapidity of the ascent easier to understand.

At that time the Sumerians seem to have been firmly established in their long hegemony of the Mesopotamia they had planted like a great garden, whose shady groves sheltered their mighty metropolises. The delights of civilization had not softened them: they remained valiant warriors. With their troops of light infantry, their heavy-armed phalanxes, and their war-chariots, they had a military machine which nothing seems to have been able to withstand. Their enemies in the field were doomed to be trampled underfoot or crushed beneath the wheels of their fighting vehicles. The 'Stele of the Vultures' and the 'Standard of Ur' illustrated such scenes, as if to warn possible opponents of the fate in store for them.

Nevertheless, the Sumerian era was about to enter the shadow of an almost total eclipse. Doubtless internal rivalries, the interminable struggles between warring cities, had already undermined the edifice. It only needed the arrival on the scene of one resolute and ambitious man for the whole structure to collapse at one blow. That man came in the person of Sargon of

Akkad (or Agade), who, at the head of his Semitic people, was to found an empire.

* * *

The period which begins with Sargon (*c.* 2475 B.C.) does not close until the time of Hammurabi of Babylon (1792-1750 B.C.). Between these two men, both of them western Semites, there takes place an attempt on the part of the Sumerians to regain their liberty and independence. Thus we shall witness the three acts of a drama which ends in the final elimination of the Sumerians. Rarely can a people so powerful, so dynamic, have been so completely liquidated. It took eight centuries of titanic struggle, carried through on the part of the Semites with the most skilful subtlety, and conducted by the Sumerians, scattered and divided by fratricidal strife though they were, with energy— but after the time of Dungi, King of Ur, with fatal nonchalance. Civilization and art could not avoid the consequences of such a struggle.

The first act is that of the Akkadians. Sargon, an officer of obscure origin, staked everything in a bid for power. He became king, founded a dynasty, and carved out for himself an empire. In 1931 there was found at Nineveh a magnificent head in bronze. It is a head of truly royal strength, its features shining with subtle intelligence. One would like to think that this is the face of King Sargon.

His grandson, Naram-Sin, carried his standards from victory to victory to maintain the heritage, setting up steles to commemorate his successes. On the stele in the Louvre (Plate 20), the deified king is leading his troops to the assault, over wooded and mountainous terrain. The gods, represented on the field of battle by their symbols, accord him a brilliant victory. Only fourteen soldiers in all are depicted on the carving, including the enemy, and yet one has the impression of seeing two armies locked in combat.

When the curtain goes up on the second act the scene has changed. The Akkadians have yielded before the onslaught of invaders sweeping down from the mountains of the north-east, the Guti. The Sumerians seize the opportunity of shaking off their chains. Their cities regain a measure of independence, for the new masters are doubtless chary of undertaking a military adventure whose benefits are by no means certain.

The great metropolises of the south, with Lagash at their head, rise swiftly to power once more. The era of the Neo-Sumerians has arrived, and it could not be better named, for in restoring the ancient traditions the Sumerians imbued them with new life. An amazing upsurge of civilization takes place. At Lagash, the modern Tello, Gudea (*c.* 2150 B.C.) covers his city with temples, and peoples it with statues. His son, Ur-Ningirsu, though perhaps less ambitious politically, nevertheless leaves for posterity a monumental hypogeum (Plates 16, 17), whither his subjects come in procession, laden with offerings. The hypogeum was bare when my workmen opened it up in 1931. But on the *via sacra* lay the votive offerings in their hundreds.

[78]

The princes of Lagash, however, were not lovers of war, or of the policy of the strong arm in their external relations; and in such matters persuasion has never been successful when not backed up by an army. It is not surprising that in such circumstances the glory of Lagash faded, as first Uruk and then Ur took the lead. The ascendancy of the Neo-Sumerians had reached its zenith. It is probable that their influence had never before been so widely felt. The great rulers of the Third Dynasty of Ur are once more in control of the entire country. Everywhere gigantic buildings are raised up in their name. Ur-Nammu, Dungi (who occupied the throne for forty-eight years) and Bur-Sin were had in awe to the farthest limits of the western world, that is to say, as far as the Mediterranean Sea. This hegemony continued unchallenged for exactly three-quarters of a century. But the position of the last two kings, Gimil-Sin and Ibi-Sin, was precarious. Once again the heritage was threatened.

We come to the third act of the Sumerian drama. The same enemies have appeared again, on the north-western borders. Successive waves of ' western Semites ', otherwise called Amorites, break through and capture the defences one by one, securing bases in the heart of the country of the Sumerians. Mari regained its independence and sent one of its chiefs, Ishbi-Irra, to occupy Isin, where he founded a dynasty (2022 B.C.). Elamite invaders took Larsa. The fabric of the power of Ur was in tatters. The fate of the town could not long be delayed. Its dynasty tottered and fell, and the last of its kings was led away captive (2016 B.C.).

Shortly afterwards, however (1894 B.C.), another Semitic dynasty was founded in Babylon. It was inevitable that this multiplicity of states should give rise to grave disorders. The Babylonians decided to gain complete control of the country, by then purely Semitic, but divided into rival kingdoms. Hammurabi (1792-1750), who combined political genius with great military skill, crushed his neighbours one by one. He was using the well-known strategy of the 'artichoke leaves', the latest illustration of which we have witnessed in the history of recent years. In this way Ashnunnak, Larsa and Mari, to mention only three of the unfortunate victims, fell one after another. Yet all three were powerful kingdoms, and sovereigns such as Ibal-pi-El, Rim-Sin and Zimri-Lim were notable warriors. All three capitals were centres of art. They were compelled to bow to the 'Babylonian peace' which installed itself among the ruins of their palaces and the wreckage of their statues. Meanwhile, upon a mountain-top, the god Shamash dictated to Hammurabi his code of two hundred and eighty-two laws.

It was this Babylonian rule, which lasted more than a century, that the patriarchs, Terah's family, fled from when they left Ur and went up to Haran, and then took the road that led them to Canaan. But in the same way as Sargon's dynasty had crumbled before the incursions of the Guti, so the dynasty of Hammurabi was to be swept away by an invasion of Kassites (sixteenth century B.C.). Both these invading peoples were barbarians, unable to adapt themselves to the refined civilization of the conquered races. Their rôle was merely to preside over the transition—for the scene was about to change.

[80]

Another great phase of Mesopotamian civilization was being ushered in: that of the Assyrians.

*   *   *

After the fall of Babylon, the inhabitants of the upper Tigris, who had always enjoyed a measure of autonomy, were forced in even more upon themselves. What took place may be described as a sort of regional crystallization around powerful cities which could already lay claim to a past that was not without its glories: around Asshur, then Kalakh (the modern Nimrud), and then Nineveh. This local hardening took place as a result of the energy of determined rulers, who gradually forged an instrument of war unrivalled in size and quality, which drew its inspiration from the experience of the past and was ready for still more audacious tasks in the future. A warlike and disciplined people, leaders with wills of iron, rigorously trained soldiers, and, finally, kings who were not over-scrupulous but who were fired with ambition, ready to risk their own persons without hesitation—here were all the conditions necessary for a bid for world conquest.

They proceeded to conquer their world, to dismember and annex it, to empty it of its wealth, to exterminate or deport its peoples. From the Persian Gulf to the Nile, all western Asia fell into the hands of the kings of Nineveh. It took them scarcely more than a century. One can follow the inexorable advance, as their dominion spread ever wider, like a patch of oil on the sea. Tiglath-pileser I (1115-1093) reached the Mediterranean; Assurnazirpal II (884-860), whose capital, Nimrud, is now being excavated by M. E. L. Mallowan, went down the coast as far as Tyre; Tiglath-pileser III (745-727), the *Pul* of the Book of Kings (II Kings 15.19) pushed as far south as Gaza, in the heart of the country of the Philistines; Shalmaneser V (727-722) laid siege to Samaria, the capital of Israel, which his successor Sargon II (722-705) finally took, in the first year of his reign. The southward march continued. In 701 Sennacherib was on the point of accomplishing the destruction of Jerusalem. But the hour of the Holy City had not yet come. The besiegers were decimated by plague and compelled to beat a retreat (II Kings 19.35). Not for long, for the soldiers of Esarhaddon (680-669), crossing the 'torrent of Egypt', penetrated for the first time in history into the Nile delta and captured Memphis. Once again the tide of conquest ebbed, only to surge back again, this time into Upper Egypt, where the army of Assurbanipal (668-626) appeared under the very walls of Thebes. The capital, the city of Amon 'that was situate among the rivers, that had the waters round about her : whose rampart was the sea [i.e. the Nile], and her wall was the waters' (Nahum 3.8, R.V. marg.), was made to submit. The victors carried away as trophies two of its obelisks. Such were the Assyrians.

It is not surprising that their art was that of a warrior people, glorifying the supreme head of the armies—the king. There is nothing graceful about this austere art. Its theme is power. The magnificent ivory mask of a woman, the 'Mona Lisa' of that distant century, discovered by Mallowan among the ruins of Nimrud in 1952, is an exception which, were it necessary, would prove the rule—but is it 'Assyrian'? This was the iron age in all its rigour, morally as well as economically. Its art is realistic, never afraid of portraying the truth, however horrible. This, it reminds us, was the age of the divine right of pillage and massacre.

This reservation made, it must be recognized that the Assyrian era was a favourable one for art. Fostered by great prosperity—all the wealth of the conquered territories was accumulated on the banks of the Tigris—Assyrian art asserted itself in every domain: architecture, sculpture, painting, metal-work and the working of precious stones. Nothing was too beautiful or too big for the huge palaces of Kalakh, Nineveh and Dur Sharrukin (now Khorsabad). Hundreds of bas-reliefs told of battles, assaults, massacres and deportations. Winged lions or bulls kept vigilant watch at the portals of the royal palaces, while on all hands rose the images of genies (Plate 15), sanctifying the deserving visitor or performing beneficent rites.

In an atmosphere thus laden with religion and steeped in sorcery, moves the hieratic figure of the king. He shows himself with his face uncovered, but before him his subjects respectfully prostrate themselves. The monarch of the greatest empire in the world presides, impassible (Plate 21), over the arrival of his tributaries, or the numbering of his captives. He listens unmoved to the report presented by his chief minister. He recruits his strength at the banquet table after risking his life on the field of battle or in the lion hunt. He offers sacrifices and pours out libations. Seemingly omnipresent, always self-sufficient, he is the lord of destiny, for the gods are with him.

Yet the wheel turns. The king is safe neither from

palace intrigues (Sennacherib was assassinated by his own son while at his devotions in a temple), nor from coalitions of his vassals. In 612, under concerted attack by Chaldeans and Medes, Nineveh is in flames. The whole of Nahum's poem recalls this unprecedented calamity. Assyria had received a mortal blow. Her death-agony lasted six years (612-606 B.C.). Once again it was Babylon's hour.

*   *   *

Babylon's return to power was brilliant but short-lived. The hegemony of the Neo-Babylonians (they have been given this name in order to distinguish them from the Amorite kings of the First Dynasty, that of Hammurabi) did not last for even one century. Well fitted to be the capital, by reason of its position at the very heart of the country, Babylon saw the restoration of its ancient temples and the aggrandizement of its palaces. Nebuchadnezzar, the conqueror of Judah (586 B.C.) and destroyer of Jerusalem and of Solomon's temple (II Kings 25), decorated the gates of his city with processions of symbolic animals: dragons, bulls and lions, recalling the three great divinities, Marduk, Adad and Ishtar. Dominating all the flat roofs of the city stood the pride of his reign, the *ziggurat* Etemenanki (the house of the foundation of heaven and earth), the 'Tower of Babel' of the Scriptures (Gen. 11). On the bank of the Euphrates, in the shady palm-grove or high up in his 'hanging gardens', the 'Chaldean' king could never forget the dangers that beset his realm, while his destiny was 'numbered, weighed, divided', in the words of the writing which appeared on the walls of Belshazzar's banqueting-hall (Dan. 5.25). The blow under which all this crumbled, in 539 B.C., was dealt by Cyrus the Achaemenid.

*   *   *

It took Cyrus and his son Cambyses twenty-five years to conquer Asia Minor, Babylon and Egypt. Darius (521-485) consolidated this great empire, making Babylon, Susa and Persepolis the three capitals of the new Achaemenid State. The Persians adopted a skilful policy, tempering their absolutism with clemency and generosity. The subject peoples kept their own laws, religions, languages and frequently their own princes. The great conquerors had utterly forgotten their own artistic traditions. They adopted those of the vanquished Assyro-Babylonians, Egyptians and (later) Greeks. The result was a composite art. These Aryan conquerors copied the bas-reliefs with their parades and processions, but they carefully eliminated from them the scenes of carnage or cruelty.

At the very most we may see the king stabbing the lion, but the torturing of prisoners, the deportations, have gone. Victory does not require these practices; the parade of tributaries, whose long tramping cohorts may be seen on the monumental staircase at Persepolis, are as eloquent a witness to the military successes of the 'King of Kings'. Around his precious person the 'immortals' keep constant watch, armed with lance and bow—the bow whose arrows had often darkened the sun.

In the palaces of the Achaemenids and in the halls of the Apadana, at both Susa and Persepolis, were columns some sixty-five feet high supporting capitals in the form of the front parts of two bulls, placed back to back. On their horns rested massive beams supporting the flat roof. The architectural reconstruction which may be seen in the Louvre (Room VII in the Department of Oriental Antiquities) is suggestive enough to make it unnecessary to describe in greater detail this colossal creation (Plate 22).

The capital is symbolic: a gigantic mass supported by a slender column. One shudders at the thought of what might happen at the first earth-tremor, at the slightest snap of rebellious Nature's fingers. That, indeed, was to come, but even swifter destruction was to come from a foreign land. It is here that Alexander makes his appearance.

*   *   *

Meanwhile, on the Anatolian plateaux and on the Phoenician sea-coast, life had progressed with a different rhythm, taking a different course. Though they may not travel the same road, it often happens that men arrive at the same point, or come to a similar stage of evolution or of progress, in spite of the perhaps widely differing geographical and political conditions which have moulded their ideas and profoundly affected all their techniques.

There could be no better example than the Hittites. They were reintroduced into history in 1906, long after the Assyrians, the Phoenicians and the Sumerians, thanks to the work of the Germans at Boghaz-Köy, Sinjirli and Sakje-Gözu; of the British at Carchemish; of the Frenchman Louis Delaporte at Malatya; of the Americans at Alishar and Tainat; and of the Turkish excavators of Kara-tepe.

The Hittites were Indo-Europeans who arrived in Anatolia in the course of the third millennium. They settled in the very heart of the country, in the loop of the Halys River, absorbing the indigenous population. They established a state, and then an ever-expanding empire which eventually spread beyond the confines of Anatolia to Syro-Phoenicia and the upper Euphrates. Theirs was a rude and even brutal civilization, a characteristic which was reinforced by the harsh nature of the country, which called for great physical resistance and sustained effort from its inhabitants. The weak were pitilessly eliminated. This sternness is the hallmark of Hittite art. Add to this the fact that the raw material at the disposal of their sculptors was basalt, the least rewarding of stones, and the clumsy appearance of some of their bas-reliefs is not hard to understand. Delicacy of execution was not possible with such a material, so that the work has a look of being unfinished, with heavy, squat silhouettes, marked nevertheless by a powerful and fiercely evocative realism (Plate 23).

Whether they are portraying the gods who wield the thunderbolt and control the storm, like the Baal found at Tell Ahmar, or the chieftain of Ivriz presiding over the reaping and the grape-harvest, the manner is always the same—powerful and massive, with the same decisive intervention of the deity who holds fecundity and

[87]

fertility in his hands. Such a deity was the object of particular veneration here where all the resources of a fundamentally hostile nature must be coaxed into service. Hence the rock-carvings of processions, the symbolic marriages, as at Yassili Kaya, in which the 'great god' comes to meet the 'great goddess', and which must necessarily bring prosperity.

Just as their political power spread down from the Anatolian plateaux, so the cultural influence of the Hittites penetrated among the surrounding populations. Near the head-waters of the Khabur, Tell Halaf, already famous for its proto-historic civilization (see above, p. 67), now furnishes a whole series of strange sculptures, going back to the twelfth-ninth centuries B.C. There are monstrous divinities, and divine monsters, enveloped in an atmosphere of terror—the terror they inspired in the hearts of their fearful worshippers. No other interpretation can be placed on the roaring lions, the being who unites in one body a bird, a man and a scorpion, to say nothing of the gigantic goddess with her square outline and her enigmatic face framed by two long plaits, the features set in defiance.

Hittite influence is not confined to this district, called the Mitanni. It extends southwards, so that Syrian art abounds in its unmistakable echoes. The lion of Sheikh Saad (Plate 24), pacing irresistibly forward, and the divine head of Jabbul, in the Louvre, are two examples of this.

Nevertheless, as soon at Hittite art leaves Anatolia, it undergoes modifications which tend to alter its character and even to remove some of its distinctive traits. The borrowings of the Assyrians and Aramaeans are not slavish copies. Damascus, at the heart of its oasis on the fringe of the desert, drew some of its artistic traditions from Egypt and from the Aegean. To remove any doubts on this score one has only to look at the sphinx carved on a stone slab found under the temple of Hadad, where the mosque of the Omayyads now stands; or to examine the fine collection of ivories discovered in 1928 at Arslan Tash, brought to his provincial residence there by Adad-nirari III (805-782 B.C.), the conqueror of Damascus.

There could scarcely be a better example of syncretism than a tradition which was inspired now by Egyptian themes (the two goddesses shielding the little Horus, the winged sphinxes), now by themes from the Aegean (the stag drinking at the stream, the cow giving suck to her calf—the latter motif actually being of Mesopotamian origin). But in the male figure standing with hands joined we see the Aramaean of the ninth century B.C. His burly strength is in sharp contrast with the lightness and grace of the themes that speak of other skies with softer horizons.

The link with those foreign climes was the western sea, over which the vessels of the Phoenicians ploughed their courses, the ‘ships of Tarshish’, well known to the prophet Jonah. Owing to its geographic unity, Phoenicia-Palestine was from the beginning a ‘turntable’ of the human race. It has been a collecting and distributing centre for thousands of years.

Economically the country was no match for the ‘great powers’, which possessed or controlled natural wealth. Of course, Phoenicia had its famous cedar-forests on the Lebanon and the Anti-Lebanon, but it lacked minerals.

Its inland plains were fertile, but they did not suffice to make the country self-supporting. The granary of the Hauran belonged to Damascus.

As for Palestine, it possessed but little timber (on Mount Carmel) and no minerals. The cultivable land, as well as being concentrated in districts where the climate was trying, allowed of only limited crops. Its coastline was difficult of access, the only port, Jaffa, being obstructed by a surf bar. Palestine had to wait until the twentieth century for a proper port—Haifa, at the foot of Mount Carmel.

Phoenicia was fortunate in having a large number of landing-places along its coast. To conquer the hinterland was out of the question, and in any case they were separated from it by the double chain of the Lebanon and the Anti-Lebanon. The Phoenicians were compelled, therefore, if they were not to sink into mediocrity, to take to the sea. Here was the chance of expansion which the land refused them. They became the world's first maritime power.

Read Chapter 27 of Ezekiel, the most vivid picture that has come down to us of the power, activity and wealth of the Phoenician port of Tyre, one of the most powerful trading centres—if not the most powerful—on the Mediterranean coast (Plate 25).

'Situate at the entry of the sea', a rallying-point on the one hand for the ships of Tarshish, and on the other for camel caravans bringing silks, spices, tissues of purple, pearls, rubies and carbuncles, wax, honey, oil and balm, wines and wool, silver, gold, iron, tin and lead, Tyre had for centuries 'filled many peoples; and enriched the kings of the earth with the multitude of its riches and of its merchandise'. Like an overloaded boat, the city had been ' broken by the seas in the depths of the waters'. Everything had been engulfed when the prophet wrote; nothing remained of Tyre but 'a bare rock . . . a place for the spreading of nets' (Ezek. 26.14).

But the Phoenicians were more than merchants and middlemen : they made themselves immortal with the invention of the alphabet. No doubt the discovery was preceded by many independent trials. Men must have been attempting over a long period to perfect the systems of writing then in use, for neither cuneiform nor hieroglyph was entirely satisfactory. After some early attempts in a writing recently termed 'pseudo-hieroglyphic', which has been deciphered, and shown to be Phoenician, by M. Edouard Dhorme, two schools of scribes arrived at a coherent system. The scribes of Ugarit had distinguished twenty-nine different simple sounds and had represented them in a cuneiform script. The Phoenicians of Byblos had gone further, with twenty-two signs only, written in an original, clear and convenient script. From then on the alphabet was fixed, and could go forward to conquer the world. Adopted and adapted by the Greeks, it passed to the Latins, who transmitted it to the West.

After a contribution of such magnitude to our universal patrimony, it seems to me to be much less important to know whether the Phoenicians showed equal originality in their art. Too many influences were coming in from the surrounding regions for it to be built up without borrowing. If, therefore, there is a Phoenician art, it is composite; but its technicians, skilled imitators as they were, succeeded in incorporating into the work of their hands that clarity and love of simplicity which goes to explain the invention of the alphabet. In Palestine, on the other hand, one ought rather to speak of artisans, more or less slavishly copying models. When some really beautiful object is recovered from the soil of Canaan, one can be pretty sure that it is either imported, or the work of a foreigner domiciled in the country and working on behalf of the indigenous inhabitants.

The exploration of Jbail-Gebal-Byblos (Plate 26), and that of Ras Shamra-Ugarit, have revolutionized our documentation on this region since the time of Renan. The excavations of Pierre Montet (1921) and M. Dunand (1926-1952) on the first site, and those of C. F. A. Schaeffer (1929-1952) on the second, have made it possible for us to have some idea of the evolution of Phoenician civilization from aeneolithic times. In both towns the successive superpositions have facilitated stratigraphical study. Although the original population is difficult to label ethnically, foreign influences are clearly traceable as soon as one arrives in historical times. Egypt manifests its presence from the Second Dynasty onwards (*c.* 2800 B.C.), with offerings from the Pharaohs in the temple at Byblos. This intercourse continued until a very late period. The Egyptians brought cargoes of papyrus, returning with resinous products.

Aegean influence appears later but is equally active. Its inspiration lies behind much of Phoenician life, as one might expect, since the country is open to the sea. In clear weather Cyprus can be seen from the Lebanese mountains.

Lastly, Asia is also present, for each of the great

inland empires sought from its inception that access to the sea which the Persian Gulf only imperfectly afforded. Long before Assyrian, Neo-Babylonian, and Persian kings successively descended the narrow coastal strip on their way towards Egypt, Sargon of Akkad had come to 'wash his weapons' in the waters of 'the upper sea' (the Mediterranean), and Hammurabi's merchants, if not his armies, had established themselves on the western coasts.

Phoenician art, then, is the product of all these factors. Synthesized harmoniously in it one finds Egypt, the Aegean, and Asia:

Egypt, with the pectorals and sarcophagus of Ahiram at Byblos, and numerous figurines and gold plaquettes at Ras Shamra;

The Aegean, with the 'teapot' and silver vase from Byblos, with certain of the themes of the golden cup and patera from Ras Shamra, and the Mycenaean ivory from the same site;

Asia, finally, with the bronze *harpés*[1] from the royal tombs at Byblos, and the stele of Baal with the thunderbolt from Ras Shamra.

These are but a few examples, where the influences are clearest. In most cases one might point to some foreign prototype, but the native hand betrays itself in some awkwardness of style or in some detail misunderstood. Nor is it rare to find the three influences together in the same object. On the famous Ras Shamra patera, which is Egyptian in form, the hunter, his chariot and

---

[1] *Translator's note*: The Greek $\check{\alpha}\rho\pi\eta$, a sickle-shaped scimitar of Mesopotamian provenance. Its use spread to Egypt, and several of the Greek heroes are depicted armed with it. Perseus, for instance, uses it to cut off Medusa's head.

his costume are Asiatic, while the general bearing of the hunted animals is strictly Aegean, directly related to the style of the Vaphio goblets.

Such were the Phoenicians. And now that from the alphabetic tablets from Ras Shamra, deciphered in record time through the united efforts of Bauer, Dhorme and Virolleaud, we are beginning to learn something of their religion, we can recreate the atmosphere of the period, with its complicated dogma, its pantheon divided by antagonisms between the various deities, its speculations, its temples and its priesthood. Numerous parallels can be drawn with the religion and the ritual of Israel, since what is coming to light at Ras Shamra is the religion and ritual of Canaan. A flood of new light has been thrown on Biblical exegesis.

So the Phoenicians—inventors, merchants, adapters, theologians and, above all, sailors—had survived every international squall. Assyrians, Neo-Babylonians and Persians had passed over them and through them in that endless descent towards Egypt. Nevertheless the Phoenician cities still stood, or, when they suffered destruction, they rose again from their ruins. But now the Orient was to be subjected to a 'new order', with the sudden manifestation of the strength of the western world.

*　　　*　　　*

The conquest of the Orient by Alexander the Great, in the fourth century B.C., marks an abrupt break in the civilization of the entire Mediterranean East, from the coasts of Phoenicia to the banks of the Indus. Like a

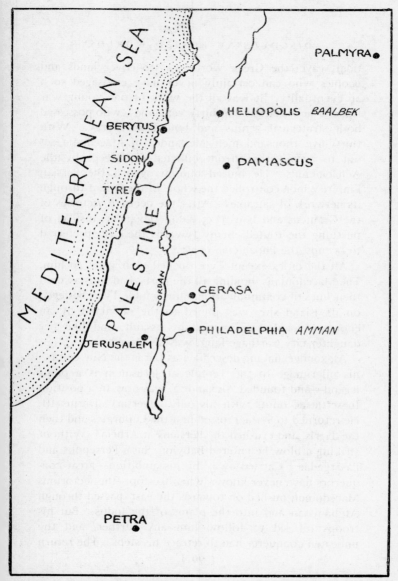

V. *Great metropolises of ancient Western Asia (before and after the beginning of the Christian era)*

tidal wave, the Greek world was to cover lands and peoples who can certainly never have envisaged such an eventuality. It was all the work of one young war leader—he was less than thirty years old—who possessed both strategical genius and boundless energy. With thirty-five thousand men Alexander of Macedonia set out to avenge the affront inflicted on Greece by the Achaemenids. He hurled himself against the Persian Empire which controlled the whole of the Orient through its network of satrapies. After the decisive victories of the Granicus and Issus (333 B.C.), Alexander, instead of pursuing the routed enemy towards the east, preferred to occupy the Phoenician coast.

All the cities except Tyre opened their gates to him. The Macedonians, holding all the ports, had thus assured their lines of communication. Intractable Tyre, besieged on its island site, was joined to the mainland by an enormous causeway, carried by assault, and like her daughter city Carthage later, was destroyed.

Alexander, having descended as far as the Nile delta—his pilgrimage to the Temple at Jerusalem is a pious legend—and founded Alexandria, was now in a position to settle accounts with his only adversary, Darius III. He returned to Syria, crossed first the Euphrates and then the Tigris, and crushed the Persians at Arbela. Without striking a blow he entered Babylon, Susa, Persepolis and Pasargadae. Carried away by his ambition—great conquerors have never known when to stop—the victorious Macedonian pushed on towards the east, passed through Afghanistan and into the plains of the Indus. But his troops refused to follow him any further, and the unbeaten conquerer had to retrace his steps. The return march was a terrible experience for all concerned. Having reached Babylon in June 323, Alexander fell sick. Ten days later he died. His empire was fated to be short-lived, but Hellenism had taken firm root in eastern soil. In a form that was doubtless decadent it presided over a widespread upsurge of artistic activity.

The hour had come in which the ancient metropolises renewed their youth in a flowing tide of new prosperity, a tide which reached the full under the tutelage of Rome, into whose lap the succession fell like a ripe fruit from the Seleucid tree.

The art which now blossomed out developed on a mass-production scale, for the sole benefit of wealthy merchants. It lasted for some five hundred years. Great cities grew up, not only on the sea-coast, like Sidon, or in the heart of a rich inland plain, like Baalbek, but also in the midst of the desert, like Palmyra, or even, in the case of Petra, in a wilderness of rocks. So, before passing too severe a judgment on this industralized art we ought to remember the audacity with which it strove, amid a hostile Nature, after grandeur and beauty. For this at least it is worthy of attention.

*   *   *

The classic example of the dominant influence of Hellenism on the Phoenician coast is furnished by the magnificent collection of sarcophagi exhumed at Sidon in 1887, now one of the finest ornaments of the Istanbul museum. The four most famous, in order of importance, are the so-called sarcophagus of Alexander, the Weeping Women, the Satrap, and the Lycian. Not everyone

[97]   **D**

would find them equally pleasing, but it is certain that practically all would agree on the excellence of the first two. That of Alexander has more sparkle, one might even say exuberance, with its scenes of warfare and hunting. The other, that of the Weeping Women, is all feeling and restrained grief. There is nothing conventional about these eighteen women, these marble sentinels alternating like living pillars with the dead columns of the temple.

The Sidon sarcophagi constitute by far the most magnificent group of funerary sculptures hitherto discovered in Phoenicia. The most impressive portion of them is, as I have said, in the Istanbul Museum. Another important collection is housed in the Beirut Museum. The Louvre, too, has a few examples, less sensational perhaps, but nevertheless of great interest. They have recently been re-arranged so that the two influences at work in Sidon may be clearly seen—the Egyptian, which is clearest in the sarcophagus of King Eshmunazar, its heavy black vat-like shape standing out against the white wall of the Marengo crypt; and the Greek, in some of the anthropoid covers, in which the masks of the dead men or women are Hellenistic in treatment.

But Sidon, as an ancient city, has almost completely disappeared. The modern city covers the Phoenician monuments. It is to the interior of the country, beyond the Lebanon range, that one must go to find the best preserved and most impressive architectural remains of that Greco-Roman syncretism which established itself on oriental soil, boldly claiming to continue the religion of Canaan by adopting its divinities, their identity scarcely altered. Thus the Baal of Baalbek became Heliopolitan Jupiter, while Hadad of Damascus reappeared as Jupiter Damascenus.

The Phoenician city of Baalbek was renamed Heliopolis after the Greek conquest. The Romans made it a centre of the cult of Jupiter, a huge temple in his honour being built there by the emperors of the second and third centuries A.D. The situation of the town is exceptional : it stands in an oasis of light and cool verdure at the foot of the Anti-Lebanon, over against Mount Lebanon to the west. Of the fifty-four columns of the temple of Jupiter only six have survived. Before the Second World War the Department of Antiquities of the High Commissioner's office found it imperative to take steps to save them from imminent collapse. With their entablatures seventeen feet high, these sixty-five feet columns stand erect like masts dominating the wreckage around them, the last mute witnesses of past glories. Turning eastwards, the visitor sees the 'little temple', incorrectly ascribed to the worship of Bacchus (Plate 27). It is far better preserved, with its walls still standing, and most of its pillars still in place, as are also many of the panels of the coffered ceiling, while the magnificent doorway remains intact. Its relatively good state of preservation makes it possible for us to visualize the proportions as well as the magnificence of the Heliopolis temples. The bronze Sursock, in the Louvre, gives us a very clear idea of the idol offered for the veneration of the faithful (Plate 29). Standing between two bulls on its pedestal, arrayed in a close-fitting cuirass, it holds the thunderbolt in its hand, the symbol of its overlordship of the elements, but also of fertility, for the water of the rainstorm brought relief from the disaster of drought.

Palmyra is the capital of the Syrian desert. 143 miles from Damascus, and 137 miles from the Euphrates, its establishment in such an inhospitable region was rendered feasible by a spring, whose waters, although sulphurous, made life possible. Palm-trees further add to the charm of this stopping-place, which the traveller reaches after crossing miles of flat desert, or, coming from the west, after journeying through a stony defile still dominated by the towers of the ancient tombs.

One comes out, almost abruptly, upon what was once Palmyra: a wide flat expanse of ruins, threaded across by long slender colonnades, all that remains of great avenues, shops and stores, temples and triumphal archways (Plate 28).

Tadmor was in existence by the beginning of the second millennium B.C. The Royal Archives of Mari contain several references to it. But its great period was of course the third century A.D., when its Queen Zenobia took it upon herself to defy Rome, which had been the suzerain of her kingdom for some 150 years. After many vicissitudes the rebellious town was finally subdued by Aurelian's troops in A.D. 272. The desert queen was taken to Rome and exhibited in the victor's triumph.

To-day Palmyra is little more than a mutilated skeleton, like that of an animal fallen by the side of the track and gnawed by beasts of prey. Yet even in its desolation it has not lost its seductive charm, for there still remains the desert setting, the tawny hill where stands a ruined Arab castle, the breeze from the oasis, the mellowed gilding of the columns, and over all the ever-changing light of the Orient, whose symphony of colours begins before dawn and does not end until after the sun has sunk behind the castle of Ibn-Ma'an.

Such was the city of Zenobia and of her subjects, rich merchants who worshipped a numerous pantheon, the chief favour of the population being reserved for the triad Bel-Yarhibol-Aglibol. Those men and women are no longer completely unknown to us, for, in countless busts and reliefs carved in soft stone, we possess their portraits—ample figures, visibly satisfied with their worldly success, great ladies richly dressed, whose effigies adorned brackets attached to the shafts of the columns or had been laid at the feet of the bodies buried in the family vaults.

Nevertheless all these triumphs, great as they are, are outclassed by the audacity of Petra. Again a desert town, it stands on the route to the Arabian peninsula. Its ancient name of Sela (rock) was well chosen. Never had a city been built amid such chaos. The capital of the land of Edom, it was despised by the Israelites. The prophet Obadiah proclaims its chastisement:

> The pride of thine heart hath deceived thee,
> thou that dwellest in the clefts of the rock, whose
>   habitation is high;
> that saith in his heart,
> Who shall bring me down to the ground?
> Though thou exalt thyself as the eagle,
> and though thou set thy nest among the stars,
> thence will I bring thee down, saith the Lord.[1]

[1] vv. 3-4.

After it fell into the hands of the Nabataeans the Edomite capital remained an obligatory halting-place for caravans plying over the Arabian peninsula. Its inhabitants had thus come to devote themselves to commerce. It was not until the first century B.C. that they sought independence, and the Aretas carved themselves out a kingdom. Rome, however, could not tolerate an autonomous native kingdom on the flank of its province of Syria, and Trajan annexed it in A.D. 106, making it the Roman province of Arabia. The city continued to enjoy great prosperity until in the third century it fell into a decline and slowly died.

To-day, wars and time have effaced practically all the dwelling-places. Only the tombs survive, cut out of the mottled sandstone of the cliff face, their façades standing out against the wild background. The town stood huddled in a great rock-girdled amphitheatre. The only approaches to it were narrow defiles, easy to guard and defend.

Driving west from Ma'an by the track which leads towards the Araba depression, the traveller comes to a valley where he must leave his car and continue on horseback; the walls of the valley gradually close in until the defile of Siq is reached. Now it is a gorge, so narrow in places that two horses cannot walk abreast. The traveller is hemmed in by two rocky walls which not only rise above him to a height of some two hundred and fifty to three hundred feet, but are often overhanging so that the sky is hidden. As one advances one is awed by the majesty with which nature is sometimes invested in its secret and privileged places.

One feels too the mystery of something superhuman.

It is as if one were out of scale with one's surroundings; as if one had passed into a land made by Titans. One feels that at any moment the giants themselves will appear.

But what does appear, after one has picked one's way slowly onward for three-quarters of an hour, like a streak of light in the narrow cleft of the defile, is the sudden façade of a funerary temple. It is known as the Khazne (the treasure) (Plate 30). The façade is carved in two storeys out of the rose-coloured stone of the cliff wall, and is richly decorated with columns, pediments and statues, the last sadly mutilated. In the lower storey a high, dark doorway opens on to the empty tomb.

A few moments later the defile widens. On the left is a theatre, whose tiers of seats have been torn from the cliff face. And then at last the broad light of the natural amphitheatre, in which stand the solitary ruins of a few buildings—temples, thermae, and a palace. On all sides rises the girdle of cliffs, pink, mauve and violet, broken by the façades of sepulchres, which, two and even three storeys high, display their alignments of columns, pilasters and pediments. On the summit of a massive sandstone hill, to the south, the high place of Zibb Atuf, preceded by its two obelisks, has remained intact with its court, its offertory table and its altar, as if waiting for the priests and the faithful to climb the steep pathway, bringing an animal for the sacrifice.

If possible one should go down once more towards the town, and there, by a spring overgrown with pink laurels, await the coming of the evening. A night spent at Petra is an unforgettable experience, especially if the moon has risen to light the other-worldly scene. The long hours of watching are no trial here, for sleeplessness, here more than anywhere else, is an invitation into the past. In such a place one understands why in so many religions the divinity has chosen the night to reveal himself to his elect.

IV

BIBLICAL PAST AND
ORIENTAL BACKGROUND

THE READER who has followed me thus far will have noticed that I have had occasion several times to make use of Biblical quotations. The fact is that one cannot dig in the soil of the Near East without coming constantly upon places and people that figure in the Old or the New Testament. A branch of oriental archaeology has thus quite naturally been devoted to Biblical archaeology.

It began on the day when Botta, digging up the palace of Khorsabad, unearthed, amid innumerable bas-reliefs, those which showed the figure of Sargon II (721-705 B.C.), the conqueror of Samaria (II Kings 17.6), and inscriptions recording in detail the deportation of the Israelites, giving the number of prisoners at twenty-seven thousand two hundred and ninety, with fifty chariots.

Shortly afterwards, the English excavator Layard found, also in Assyria, some even more important bas-reliefs, depicting Shalmaneser III (858-824 B.C.) receiving tribute from Jehu, King of Israel (I Kings 19.16; II Kings 9 and 10), and Sennacherib besieging, in 701 B.C., the Palestinian town of Lachish (II Kings 18).

Of course, the seven-branched candlestick and the table for the shew-bread, from Herod's Temple at Jerusalem, were already known from the Arch of Titus at

Rome. But this dated only from a comparatively late period (A.D. 70). The Assyrian reliefs took archaeology a big step back—eight and nine centuries before Christ —to the time of the conquerors of Israel so often spoken of by the great prophets. This, however, was only the beginning. The interest aroused in England by these discoveries was increased by the Assyriologist George Smith's sensational announcement in 1872 that he had deciphered a cuneiform version of the Deluge story.[1]

These were but the first of a whole series of discoveries, made on many different sites.

In 1871 Clermont-Ganneau recovered at Jerusalem an inscribed block, built into the wall of an enclosure. It bore an inscription in Greek by Herod the Great, intended to be placed in the interior of the Temple. It warned strangers against crossing a certain boundary, on pain of death. It makes it much easier to understand the passage in Acts (21.29) in which Paul is accused of having brought Trophimus the Ephesian into the Temple, thus formally violating the Herodian regulation.

Five years earlier, in 1866, a votive foot, bearing the name 'Pompeia Lucilia', had been found not far from the *piscina probatica* at Jerusalem—an offering to commemorate a cure. So the paralytic of John 5 might also properly expect an improvement in his condition.

In 1873 the Louvre, thanks again to Clermont-Ganneau, acquired the stele of Mesha, King of Moab, the 'sheepmaster' (II Kings 3.4) and great adversary of Israel.

In 1880 a rock-inscription was found at the mouth of

---

[1] A detailed account of this event will be found in *The Flood and Noah's Ark, Studies in Biblical Archaeology*, No. 1 (SCM Press, London, 1955).

the canal of Siloam, giving an account of the cutting of the channel, no doubt by Hezekiah, for II Kings 20.20 is explicit on the subject: 'The rest of the acts of Hezekiah . . . and how he made a pool, and a conduit, and brought water into the city. . . .'

In 1893, this time at Thebes, in Egypt, Flinders Petrie discovered in the funerary temple of Pharaoh Meneptah (1234-1224) a stele, now often called the 'Israel stele', since it bears the first and only reference in Egypt to Israel, in connection with one of the Pharaoh's campaigns.

In 1887, also in Egypt, at El Amarna, the capital of the heretical Pharaoh Akhnaton, there came to light diplomatic correspondence, written in cuneiform, containing, among others, letters written from governors resident in Phoenicia, Southern Syria and Palestine, in the fifteenth and fourteenth centuries B.C. The collection contains three hundred and seventy-seven texts, nearly three hundred of them letters, including several from Abdu-Hepa, Governor of Jerusalem.

Thus, one after another, the three Biblical countries, Mesopotamia, Palestine and Egypt, were beginning to give up their secrets, although as yet no one guessed how much was to follow. What was known had first to be catalogued and classified. In 1909 Hugo Gressmann published his *Altorientalische Texte und Bilder zum Alten Testament*,[1] while two British Assyriologists who had been working on the Nineveh texts introduced the

---

[1] A work of one hundred and forty pages, with text and plates in one volume, completely recast in the second edition, which has separate volumes for text (pp. x, 478) and plates (CCLX) (1926-1927). The work continues: in 1950 James B. Pritchard published *Ancient Near Eastern Texts Relating to the Old Testament* (pp. xxi, 526). A volume of plates is in preparation.

general public to those which related to the Bible. *The Seven Tablets of Creation*, by L. W. King, appeared in 1902.

The same year saw the beginning of a bitter controversy. On 13th January 1902 Friedrich Delitzsch delivered before Kaiser Wilhelm II a lecture entitled *Babel und Bibel*, which caused widespread interest. Some saw it as an arrogant challenge, whereas the speaker, rising above the domain of pure archaeology, had finished by raising the debate to the spiritual plane, as he called to witness the long line of prophets and psalmists who prepared the way for the preaching of Jesus and the worship of God 'in spirit and in truth'. Delitzsch had, of course, taken up a definite position, but it is possible now to see that it was a very moderate one. As often happens, his followers were much more intransigent than their master. In spite of the numerous school of the Pan-Babylonists, the position of the exegetists, chief among whom were Graff and Wellhausen, did not seem to be seriously threatened. It appeared now that the science of the Old Testament must be fixed on bases where not many new surprises were to be expected.

From then onwards all the great nations were represented in the Near East or in Palestine, through one or more organizations engaged in exploration or in study of the documents already recovered. It is interesting to note here the dates of the foundation of the various Schools and Institutes. In 1869, the Palestine Exploration Fund; in 1892 the *Ecole Biblique* of the Dominicans of Saint-Etienne, of which the first director was Père Séjourné, followed by Père Lagrange; in 1898, the

Deutsche Orient-Gesellschaft, simultaneously in Palestine and Mesopotamia (excavations at Babylon and Asshur); in 1900, the American Schools of Oriental Research; in 1901, the *Deutsches Evangelische Institut für Altertumskunde*. Thus, by the beginning of the twentieth century, British, French, Germans and Americans were on the spot and at work.

I have already said that the First World War marked a decisive break in archaeological work. As soon as the armistice was signed the work began again, at an ever-increasing pace, as if those engaged in it were conscious of the inevitability, and then of the imminence, of a second world war, and of the need for haste. A few examples will show the quality of the magnificent harvest that was reaped.

First of all, improved techniques were applied to systematic digging on Palestinian sites: Jerusalem (in spite of the difficulties caused by the fact that the ancient city lies buried under many feet of debris, and under modern dwellings which cannot be demolished), Jericho (previously explored, but badly), Beth-el, Ai, Megiddo, Samaria, Capernaum and Lachish. On this last site (now Tell Duwair) were found *ostraka* bearing inscriptions in ink, among which were remarkable parallels recalling the atmosphere of the period preceding the destruction of Jerusalem (586 B.C.), and containing explicit references to a certain prophet of misfortune, whom many were tempted to identify with the prophet Jeremiah.[1]

But Palestine was comparatively unfruitful—although the discoveries of 1947-1952 will make it necessary to

[1] One of the *Studies in Biblical Archaeology* will be devoted to this subject.

reconsider this judgment—never furnishing more than the merest shreds of evidence. Yet, even in their desolation, the stones cry out.

For several years, therefore, it was beyond the boundaries of Palestine that the most important discoveries bearing on the Scriptures were made. From 1929 to 1939 interest was centred on Ras Shamra, with its mythological tablets of the fourteenth century B.C., its statuettes of Baals and Astartes, and the god El, whom we already knew from Old Testament texts, though the importance of these references is only now being realized.

Between 1936 and 1939 I recovered from the palace at Mari several thousand cuneiform tablets (eighteenth century B.C.) which constituted the Royal Archives of the city. Here light was thrown on the patriarchal period. Specifically Biblical names, such as Nahor and Haran, occur, and mention is made of the Habiru and of Benjamites. Speaking of the decipherment of these texts the American orientalist W. F. Albright writes: 'The latest discoveries at Mari on the Middle Euphrates . . . have strikingly confirmed the Israelite traditions according to which their Hebrew forefathers came to Palestine from the region of Harran.'[1]

I could go on to show also, for example, the extraordinary correspondence between the Nuzi tablets and the patriarchal customs (the subject will be dealt with at greater length elsewhere), or how the recent reading of Sumerian texts has revealed impressive parallels with the early chapters of Genesis (the Creation, Eden, the Fall). This also deserves a detailed study, for it would

[1] *From the Stone Age to Christianity*, p. 179.

not be right to treat superficially subjects of such vital importance for mankind.[1]

I must now draw some of the conclusions which justify (if justification is necessary) the position which I have long held, and to which I still adhere.

With the carvings, statues and texts discovered among the ruins of the cities explored by the archaeologists, the whole history of the ancient world lies revealed, like a mummy found intact amid its wrappings in the tomb. The light cast upon secular history fell inevitably on the Bible also, so that on all sides the cry went up : 'Thanks to archaeology, the truth of the Bible has been completely vindicated.'[2] This well-intentioned though sometimes imprudent enthusiasm at once aroused a reaction on the part of sceptics, who asserted just as categorically : 'Archaeology, while perhaps confirming certain historical facts, has been unable to do more than that. Above all, it has never proved that in those facts God was really and truly revealing Himself.'

We are not called upon to choose between these two opposing views, though each has at times been even vehemently upheld, for both are extreme. The first is the result of an over-hasty appreciation of a documentation which has increased beyond the grasp of any single mind, and which, even for the specialist, has made old problems more complex and more delicate. The second view, based on an obvious *a priori* assumption, evinces an utter misunderstanding of the results obtained. It is

---

[1] I shall be dealing in detail with all these subjects in the series of *Studies in Biblical Archaeology*.

[2] Sir C. Marston : *The Bible is True*, Eyre and Spottiswoode, London, 1934.

curious indeed to note that now scepticism, or, if it is preferred, reserve, in this field is no longer the prerogative of the agnostics, but is actually the attitude of a large number of theologians and exegetists. The precision of archaeology frightens them, for it compels them to view somewhat differently the process of Revelation. The reaction provoked in certain circles by my book *Ziggurats et Tour de Babel* is a striking example of this. There is no need to mention the Ras Shamra tablets, which others have found disturbing. I shall be returning elsewhere to this subject as well, for I am more than ever convinced that archaeology, so far from making difficulties, in fact removes them all, so long as one does not distort any of the facts revealed on the excavation sites.

Let me then in this connection sum up what it is that in my opinion archaeology has to tell us. Firstly, it has confirmed *historical facts*. As is well known, certain currents of theological thought profess towards history an attitude almost of disdain. According to them, precise facts concerning the behaviour of individuals have only a very minor importance. It is therefore pointless to attempt to give an exact date, or to go more closely into some train of political events. What matters, we are told, is the Word, and the Word alone. But how are we to understand it without setting it against its proper chronological, historical and geographical background? How are blunders to be avoided if our interpretation treats a given situation completely *in vacuo*, and without first attempting to define its exact contours? Some fifteen years ago Eissfeldt wrote that the theological use of the Old Testament depended on a historical understanding of it, and that this could be acquired only by setting the Old Testament against its background. This is the attitude of many Old Testament scholars (the work of Professor H. H. Rowley of Manchester is an example), but there is at least one illustrious precedent for it—one that is difficult to challenge.

Luke the physician—I quote his example, for it seems to me to be conclusive—evidently did not consider history unimportant. He established the exact point in time and space at which the Word of God came to John in the desert. It is well to recall this exordium, which advances like a solemn cortège: 'Now in the fifteenth year of the reign of Tiberius Caesar, Pontius Pilate being governor of Judaea, and Herod being tetrarch of Galilee, and his brother Philip tetrarch of Ituraea and of the region of Trachonitis, and Lysanias the tetrarch of Abilene, Annas and Caiaphas being the high priests, the word of God came unto John the son of Zacharias in the wilderness' (Luke 3.1-2). Luke, then, considered history and geography to be vital elements. All these places and personages had first to be set in position before the Word came to the son of Zacharias.

Although archaeology has confirmed historical facts beyond the possibility of doubt (perhaps one of the most striking examples is the discovery at Babylon of cuneiform tablets listing the rations delivered to certain captives, including 'Ja'ukin, king of the land of Jahudu' —clearly Jehoiachin, king of Jerusalem and Judah, deported in 597 B.C., as is recorded in II Kings 24.12), it would be rash to suppose that it has *always* demonstrated the scrupulous accuracy of *every* historical particular preserved in the Scriptures. A single example :

the town of Ai can scarcely have been taken by Joshua
(Josh. 7-8), for digging has revealed that the city had
been destroyed long before the arrival of the Israelites.
Its site was indeed a 'ruin' (this is precisely what *Ai*
means), but it is difficult to believe that the ruin was
occupied by a king! Nevertheless a king is mentioned
(Josh. 8.1). Inexactitudes over details there certainly
are, which of course do not detract from the 'sub-
stantial' truth of the historical tradition of the Old
Testament, but which we have no right to pass over
in silence.

Secondly, archaeology has established the exact loca-
tion of places. Jesus, indeed, did once say: 'Blessed are
they that have not seen, and yet have believed.' That
saying is for all those, the great majority, who have not
had and never will have the privilege of treading the
soil of Palestine. But Jesus also said: 'Blessed are the
eyes which see the things that ye see.'

The sites once rediscovered and located on the ground,
it seems that the Revelation becomes more tangible, for
we are men, and we need these landmarks, these stations,
where we can pause and meditate. Thanks to archaeology there are thus in Palestine definite spots where one
can say in all certainty that in walking there some two
thousand years after Jesus, one is treading where He
trod.

At Capernaum the synagogue has been reconstructed
on the site of the temple of Gospel times. At the foot of
Mt. Gerizim, in the gap of Sichem, are to be seen
(though, alas, enclosed in an unfinished church) the well
of Jacob and its thirst-quenching water 'near to the
parcel of ground that Jacob gave to his son Joseph'

(John 4.5). At Jerusalem, on the hill of Sion, there is a staircase whose existence had long been unsuspected, going down towards Siloam and the brook Cedron. Was it perhaps used that last evening? And lower down, where from time immemorial the Jews have buried their dead, are the sepulchres of the righteous (Matt. 23.29) which Jesus could see from the terrace of the Temple, and by the foot of which He must certainly have passed on the first Maundy Thursday evening on His way to the garden of Gethsemane. And, lastly, thanks to archaeology, we have a fragment of Herod's city-wall, and in it the threshold of the gate through which Jesus must have been led out of the city to be crucified.

But archaeology has done more than confirm secular or sacred history and rediscover its sites. It has restored to us the soul of those vanished peoples itself, by revealing in the documents dug from the soil their way of life. It shows us the God of Revelation at work. 'At sundry times and in divers manners'—everywhere the truth of this affirmation by the author of the Epistle to the Hebrews is brought home, for God has spoken everywhere, not always in the same language, but always with the same accent.

But while God was seeking out men, men too were in search of God. From the remotest times we have seen humanity concerned with symbols that bear witness to definite beliefs. By laying 'funerary furniture' near the bodies of their dead the Mesopotamians implicitly affirmed their belief in an after-life. This earth is not all. There is something to follow.

The Graff-Wellhausen school postulated the following evolutionary scheme: animism, polytheism, henotheism, monotheism. Archaeology, however, furnishes no evidence of animism, but, on the contrary, attests from the earliest times belief in divinities. The temples of Gawra and Eridu, the statuettes from Jericho and the figurines from Jarmo are the architectural and sculptural illustrations of these initial beliefs.

Consequently, we witness the existence from the beginning of a two-fold current, a traffic between earth and heaven. At Beth-el, in a dream, Jacob beheld a ladder set up, and the angels of God ascending and descending on it (Gen. 28.12).

This dialogue between heaven and earth was neverending. Yet it had its troubles, and the record, in which everything might have been light, is interleaved with shadows and with blood. Some readers of the Old Testament have found, and still find, certain of its pages scandalous. Why scandalous? Archaeology intervenes once more, revealing the Biblical world in its entirety—by which is meant no longer Palestine only, but also Mesopotamia, Syria, Phoenicia and Egypt. By bringing us dated documents from all these peoples and races, among whom Israel is only a tiny island, it enables us to make comparisons and contrasts which explain and clarify everything. If we set Israel against the background of the period, there is no longer any risk of our being shocked or put out by anything the Bible has to say. Firstly, because the Bible shows us men as they are and as they were. Secondly, because we find evidence elsewhere of the same imperfections and the same mistaken ideas. We must frankly recognize those imperfections, those mistakes, even those crimes; and we must not interpret them in terms of an extravagant and exaggerated symbolism. 'The stones cry out.' Let them cry, but let us scrupulously respect what has been called their 'frank speech'.

After the Patriarchs, after Moses, the Kings and the Prophets, the hour had come : everything was ready for the supreme Revelation. And now Biblical archaeology's latest discovery : among the scrolls from a cave near the Dead Sea orientalists have found a complete manuscript of the Book of Isaiah, fifty-four columns of text on seventeen sheets of parchment sewn together end to end. Doubtless it was just such a roll that was handed in the synagogue of Nazareth to Jesus, for Him to unroll and read (Luke 4.16-17). We are brought nearer to every gesture of Jesus of Nazareth, for on the back of the parchment can still be seen the marks left by the fingers of the readers. This manuscript, hidden shortly before the Jewish War, some forty years after the death of Jesus, thus furnishes us with what is surely the most striking and intimate illustration of one of the acts of the Son of Man, witnessing also to the accomplishment of the prophecy He had just read to His unbelieving countrymen, written in just such a hand as this parchment has preserved for us to read, some two thousand years later.

SIC TRANSIT GLORIA MUNDI

CLOSE by the hill of *Babil* runs the railway linking Baghdad and Basra. A wooden board at the side of the line announces simply: 'Babylon Halt. Trains stop here to pick up passengers.' The traveller has arrived at Babylon, and his first impression of what was once the greatest capital of the ancient world is that placard. Not even a station—merely a 'halt'!

There could surely be no better illustration of the fate of those old empires, 'great ships, loaded with riches and vitality', swallowed up with all they possessed. Such is the ineluctable law which governs nations and civilizations equally with individuals. They are caught in the great mill and ground to dust.

In the face of this vast theatre of time, where actor follows actor across the ever-changing scene, what is man? When the curtain has fallen, a little heap of white dust, which one cannot handle without thinking of the offering of struggles, of suffering—of love, too, that it represents.

Such are the visible and perishable remains which I have spent the last twenty-five years restoring to the light of day. They have played their part, and for them the drama is ended. Yet time has not stopped, but flows tirelessly on, the same water in the same great river, irresistibly carving out its channel through every

[118]

obstacle. None can foretell where or when the end will come. In the eyes of the eternal God a thousand years are as one day—and at every hour of each of those days, men rise up, move forward, and then crumble away. Their flesh is as grass, and all the goodliness thereof is as the flower of the field : the words are those of Isaiah, who goes on : 'The grass withereth, the flower fadeth, but the word of our God shall stand for ever.' This is the message for our time that comes to us from the remotest depths of history, from the very heart of the buried worlds.

BIBLIOGRAPHY

SPACE does not allow me to do more than indicate a few recent publications written by specialists. They are grouped according to the subject-matter of the chapters of the present work.

CHAPTER I. Several excavators have brought to life the atmosphere of the sites: C. L. Woolley, *Digging up the Past*, Ernest Benn, London, 1930; Bohtz, *In den Ruinen von Warka*, 1941; C. H. Gordon, *The Living Past*, 1941; A. Parrot, *Villes enfouies*, Paris, 1934; *Mari, une ville perdue*, 4th edition, Paris, 1948.

I have dealt in detail with Mesopotamian excavation in *Archéologie mésopotamienne*, Vol. II; *Technique et Problèmes*, which includes a bibliography of the subject (pp. 101-103).

CHAPTER II. For the history of the excavations: Seton Lloyd, *Foundations in the Dust*, O.U.P., London, 1947; A. Parrot, *Archéologie mésopotamienne*, Vol. I; *Les étapes* (out of print, but to be reprinted). For Palestine and Phoenicia: Hennequin, *Fouilles et champs de fouilles en Palestine et en Phénicie*, in the *Supplément au Dictionnaire de la Bible*, 1936; this must, of course, be supplemented, for example with C. C. McCown, *The Ladder of Progress in Palestine*, Harper & Bros., New York and London, 1943. A general account of the Near-

[121]

Eastern sites and their stratigraphical relationships in
C. F. A. Schaeffer, *Stratigraphie comparée et chronologie
de l'Asie occidentale, IIIe et IIe millénaires*, O.U.P., London, 1948.

CHAPTER III. For the great periods of civilization and
art, numerous manuals and articles. A few titles only :
G. Contenau, *Manuel d'archéologie orientale*, 4 vols.,
Paris, 1927-1947; in the series *Peuples et civilisations*,
Vol. I, *Peuples et civilisations*, 1950, with chapters by
E. Dhorme and G. Contenau. I have dealt in detail with
Mesopotamian proto-history in *Archéologie mésopo-
tamienne*, Vol. II, pp. 107-331.

For Palestine, A. G. Barrois, *Manuel d'archéologie
biblique*, I, 1939; II, 1953.

For Byblos, works by P. Montet and M. Dunand; for
Ras Shamra, those of Schaeffer (Ugaritica, I & II, 1939,
1949) and Virolleaud.

The relation of Egypt to the Bible has received much
less systematic study than that existing between the
Bible and Mesopotamia or between the Bible and Syria
and Palestine. A detailed bibliography will be given in
the *Studies* dealing with the relation of Egypt to the
Bible. Meanwhile, the reader will find occasional refer-
ences in the volumes by Albright (*Archaeology and the
Religion of Israel*, new edition, 1953; and *From the Stone
Age to Christianity*, of which a new version has been
announced for 1954/55) or by Rowley (*From Joseph to
Joshua*). The earlier works need to be supplemented in
several important respects : for example, E. Naville,
Archaeology of the Old Testament, 1911; G. A. Barton,
Archaeology and the Bible, American Sunday-School

Union, Philadelphia, 7th ed., 1937; *The Haverford Symposium on Archaeology and the Bible*, Haverford College and the American Schools of Oriental Research, 1938. Mention should also be made of the still excellent work of P. Humbert, *Recherches sur les sources égyptiennes de la littérature sapientale d'Israël*, Neuchâtel, 1929.

For Near-Eastern art, important chapters will be found in the Histories of Art recently published or prepared by numerous publishing-houses, for instance, Flammarion, *Histoire générale de l'art*, Vol. I, 1950, or Gallimard (in course of publication). Considerable space is given to ancient western Asia in the latest works of André Malraux, *Les voix du silence*, 1951, and *Le musée imaginaire de la sculpture mondiale*, 1952.

CHAPTER IV. Increasing attention is being paid to the bearing of archaeology on the Bible. I shall give later a detailed bibliography of the subjects with which it is proposed to deal in the *Studies in Biblical Archaeology*.

In America: M. Burrows, *What mean these Stones?*, American Schools of Oriental Research, 1941; G. E. Wright and F. V. Filson, *The Westminster Historical Atlas to the Bible*, 1945; J. Finegan, *Light from the Ancient Past*, Princeton U.P., Princeton, 1946; W. F. Albright, *Archaeology and the Religion of Israel*, John Hopkins Press, Baltimore, new ed., 1953; *From the Stone Age to Christianity*, John Hopkins Press, 1946; *The Archaeology of Palestine*, Penguin Books, 1949; G. E. Wright, 'Biblical Archaeology To-day', in *The Biblical Archaeologist*, XI, 1947, pp. 7-24 (an excellent periodical).

In England, the numerous works of H. H. Rowley, *The*

Re-Discovery of the Old Testament, James Clarke & Co., London, 1946; *From Joseph to Joshua*, O.U.P., London, 1950; (editor) *The Old Testament and Modern Study*, Society for Old Testament Study, 1951; *The Servant of the Lord*, Lutterworth Press, London, 1952; and those of S. H. Hooke, T. H. Robinson, G. R. Driver, S. A. Cook, A. R. Johnson. A valuable bibliography appears in the *Book List* published annually by the Society for Old Testament Study.

In France, I shall mention only three authors: R. Dussaud, *Les découvertes de Ras Shamra (Ugarit) et l'Ancien Testament*, Paris, 1941; E. Dhorme, *Recueil Edouard Dhorme, Etudes bibliques et orientales*, 1951, a collection of the most important articles written by this scholar 'over nearly half a century'; C. F. Jean, *Le milieu biblique avant Jésus-Christ*, I-III, 1922-1936, containing a wealth of documents and information which needs in certain cases, however, to be brought up to date to take account of recent discoveries and new readings.

It would be impossible to omit here the complete collection of the *Revue biblique* of the Dominicans of St.-Etienne, who have always been in the forefront of Palestinian archaeology; and many of the issues of the *Revue d'histoire et de philosophie religieuses* (articles by E. Jacob), and of the *Revue de l'histoire des religions* (*Semitica*).

In Germany several authors have devoted considerable attention to archaeology: A. Alt, I. Benzinger (*Hebräische Archäologie*, 1894), O. Eissfeldt (*Der Gott Karmel*, 1953), K. Galling (*Biblisches Reallexikon*, 1934), M. Noth (*Mari und Israel*, 1953), H. Schmökel.

BIBLIOGRAPHY

In Switzerland: P. Humbert, in Neuchâtel, and W. Baumgartner, in Basle, make frequent use of the discoveries of archaeology.

In Scandinavia and Holland: J. Coppens, de Langhe, F. M. T. de Liagre Böhl (*Opera Minora*, 1953), van der Ploeg, A. Bentzen (d. 1953), J. Pedersen, J. Engnell, writing from varying theological standpoints, rely frequently on Near-Eastern archaeology. In this connection mention should be made of the review recently founded (1951) at Leyden, *Vetus Testamentum*, in particular a collection published by it after the Congress of Copenhagen under the title *Congress Revue* (1953).

Finally, two collections that are indispensable to Biblical students: H. Gressmann, *Altorientalische Texte zum Alten Testament*, 1926, *Altorientalische Bilder zum Alten Testament*, 1927; J. B. Pritchard (and others), *Ancient Near Eastern Texts Relating to the Old Testament*, Princeton U.P., Princeton, 1950.

STUDIES IN BIBLICAL ARCHAEOLOGY

The first titles in this series, which are uniform in appearance, with plentiful maps and illustrations, and cost approximately 7s. 6d. each, are

1. *The Flood and Noah's Ark*
2. *The Tower of Babel*
3. *Nineveh and the Old Testament*
4. *St. Paul's Journeys in the Greek Orient*
   by Henri Metzger
5. *The Temple of Jerusalem*
6. *Golgotha and the Church of the Holy Sepulchre*

Later titles will include *Mari and the Old Testament, The Dead Sea Scrolls, Ur of the Chaldees, The Exodus.*

Except where indicated, the author of each monograph is André Parrot.

[126]

INDEX

[127]